MARXISM/SOCIALISM, A SOCIOPATHIC PHILOSOPHY CONCEIVED IN GROSS ERROR AND IGNORANCE, CULMINATING IN ECONOMIC CHAOS, ENSLAVEMENT, TERROR, AND MASS MURDER: A CONTRIBUTION TO ITS DEATH

GEORGE REISMAN

TJS Books, Laguna Hills, California

MARXISM/SOCIALISM, A SOCIOPATHIC PHILOSOPHY CONCEIVED IN GROSS ERROR AND IGNORANCE, CULMINATING IN ECONOMIC CHAOS, ENSLAVEMENT, TERROR, AND MASS MURDER: A CONTRIBUTION TO ITS DEATH

George Reisman, Ph.D., is Pepperdine University Professor Emeritus of Economics and the author of *Capitalism: A Treatise on Economics* (Ottawa, Illinois: Jameson Books, 1996; Kindle Edition, 2012). See his Amazon.com author's page. His website is www.capitalism.net. His blog is www.georgereismansblog.blogspot.com. Follow him on Twitter @GGReisman.

Published by TJS BOOKS, PO Box 2934, Laguna Hills, CA 92654.

Copyright © 2018 by George Reisman, All rights reserved.

ISBN: 9781723785078

All inquiries should be addressed to TJS Books, PO Box 2934, Laguna Hills, CA 92654-2934 or to TJS.Books@capitalism.net. Phone: (877) 843-3573. Fax: (949) 831-1783.

See below, after the "Summary" and "Conclusion," the section "Royalty-Free Distribution of Copies."

In memoriam for my late wife Edith Packer, J.D., Ph.D., without whose forty-eight-plus years of companionship neither this nor any other important publication of mine would have been possible.

This page intentionally left blank.

Table of Contents

Introduction 1

PART I. THE GIST OF MARXISM/SOCIALISM AND ITS REFUTATION 5

I. 1. The Essential Nature of Socialism: The Need for Armed Robbery to Establish It 5

I. 2. The Social Democrats Should Stop Calling Themselves Socialists 6

I. 3. The Marxists/Socialists' Rationalization for the Armed Robbery Needed to Establish Socialism: Alleged "Exploitation" and "Wage Slavery" under Capitalism 7

I. 4. The Essential Difference between Free Labor and Slave Labor that Marxism/Socialism Ignores 10

I. 5. Adam Smith as the Father of the Marxian Exploitation Theory 12

I. 6. Marx's "Simple Circulation" and "Capitalistic Circulation" 14

I. 7. Profits, Not Wages, as the Original and Primary form of Labor Income 15

I. 8. Capitalists Responsible for Wages, Costs, and Reduction of Profits 18

I. 9. Profits Still an Income Earned by the Labor of Capitalists 21

I. 10. Passive Capitalists 25

I. 11. The Irrelevance of "Worker Need" and "Employer Greed" in the Determination of Wages 26

I. 12. Marxism/Socialism as an Underlying Cause of Unemployment and Why the Fall in Wage Rates Required to Eliminate It Need Not Reduce Real Wages 39

I. 13. How Capitalism Progressively Raises Real Wages 42

I. 14. How Capitalism Shortens the Working Day, Abolishes Child Labor, and Improves Working Conditions 48

I. 15. Implication of Harmful Effects of Government Interference with Hours and Conditions of Work 51

I. 16. Fallacy of the Marxists'/Socialists' Belief that to Benefit from the Means of Production, People Need to Own Them 52

I. 17. How Capitalism Is Run for the Benefit of the Masses while Socialism Is Run for the Benefit of the Ruling Elite at the Cost of Starvation Wages 55

I. 18. Fallacy of the Marxists'/Socialists' Belief that Capitalism Lacks Planning and Is an "Anarchy of Production" 57

I. 19. Enslavement under Socialism 62

I. 20. The Necessity of Terror under Socialism 64

I. 21. From Enslavement to Mass Murder under Socialism 68

PART II. MARX'S LABOR THEORY OF VALUE LUNACY 71

II. 1. What Marx Ignores to Get to His Labor Theory of Value and the Exploitation Theory 71

II. 2. The Implication that the Product of an Hour's Labor by a Brain Surgeon Has the Same Value as that of an Hour's Labor by a Gardener, and the Dishonesty of Marx's Attempt to Defend this Absurd Claim 72

II. 3. Further Implications: Only Fresh Labor Adds Value and the Value of Labor Itself Is Determined by the Quantity of Labor Required to Produce It 73

II. 4. Marx's Claim that Subsistence Wages Are Permanent under Capitalism 75

II. 5. Marx's Unintended Concession Concerning the Economic Role of Capitalists and His Delusional Interpretation of It 78

II. 6. Marx's Claim of Progressive Impoverishment: Capitalists' Greed and a Falling Rate of Profit 79

II. 7. The Absurdity of Marx's Proposition that only the Wage-Paying Part of Capital Yields Profit 80

II. 8. Marx's Claim that the Capitalists' Greed and a Falling Rate of Profit Result in an Increase in the Rate of Exploitation and in the Length of the Working Day 82

II. 9. Marx's Claim Concerning the Capitalists' Appropriation of the Labor of Women and Children Through the Use of Machinery 84

II. 10. An Additional Absurd Claim by Marx: Cheapening the Worker's Diet 86

Part III. THE ACTUAL DETERMINANTS OF PROFIT AND THE RATE OF PROFIT 89

III. 1. The Prime Cause of Profit: Expenditure to Buy Commodities 90

III. 2. The Origin of Costs to be Deducted from Sales Revenues 91

III. 3. Productive Expenditure, Sales Revenues, and Costs 92

III. 4. Productive Expenditure, Costs, and Net Investment 94

III. 5. The Tendency toward Productive Expenditure and Income-Statement Costs Becoming Equal 95

III. 6. Net Consumption: The Excess of Sales Revenues over Productive Expenditure 98

III. 7. Net Investment and Its Disappearance 101

III. 8. Increases in the Quantity of Money and the Perpetuation of Net Investment 103

III. 9. The Rate of Increase in the Quantity of Money as a Determinant of the Rate of Profit 104

III. 10. Marxism's/Socialism's Conflict of Hatreds 106

SUMMARY AND CONCLUSION 109

ROYALTY-FREE DISTRIBUTION OF COPIES 115

ACKNOWLEDGEMENTS 117

POSTSCRIPT 119

NOTES 123

Introduction

On April 30 of this year [2018], *The New York Times* ran an op-ed piece titled "Happy Birthday, Karl Marx. You Were Right!"[1] In view of the fact that the implementation of Marx's philosophy in the Soviet Union and in Communist China resulted in general economic chaos, including shortages, rationing, interminable waiting lines (14 hours a week just to buy food), and multiple families having to live in the same apartment, plus forced labor, concentration camps, show trials and periodic purges to shift the blame for it all, a reign of terror, famines, and as many as 62 million murders in the Soviet Union and 76 million in Communist China (including those killed by the government-caused famines)[2]—in view of all this, congratulating Marx on being right boggles the mind. Marx could be right only if one's standard of right was human misery and death. Only someone utterly depraved could make such a statement. Only an utterly depraved, despicable newspaper could endorse such a statement, and the feather-weight rationalizations offered in support of it, by printing the piece.

In every essential respect, the philosophy of Marxism/Socialism is a philosophy designed for sociopaths—for people who attempt to appear merely as seeking to do good, by posturing as friends of the poor and of humanity at large, but who have no respect for the individual rights of others, who have no awareness that others have independent minds and think and plan on their own initiative, who denounce such thinking and planning as "anarchy" (an "anarchy of production") and try to squelch it, who regard others as mere objects to be willingly or unwillingly manipulated in the achievement of the Marxists'/Socialists' grand plans for the human race, and whose response to the suffering and deaths of millions is along the lines of "to make an omelet, you have to break some eggs." Marxism/Socialism is a philosophy for the depraved, for those of a warped intellectual and moral capacity and thus capable of appearing now as morons and now as murderers. It is a philosophy designed for a special breed of such vermin: for those who, despite often thinking at the level of morons, nevertheless believe that they are more intelligent than other people, so much more intelligent in fact, that they know better how to run other people's lives than those other people themselves do and are entitled to use force to impose their will on them. Marxism/Socialism is the philosophy of a breed of mental cases whose ignorance is exceeded only by its arrogance and viciousness.

The *Times'* endorsement of Marx was not an isolated event. In June, a New York State Democratic congressional primary was won by a member of the Democratic Socialists of America, an organization that has grown rapidly since the presidential candidacy of the self-described socialist Sen. Bernie Sanders. Sanders' candidacy has been followed by a resurgence of socialism both on college campuses and in the Democratic Party. It has gone so far in the Democratic Party that former FBI Director James Comey, a current supporter of the Democrats, has believed it necessary to tweet, "Democrats, please, please don't lose your minds and rush to the socialist left."

The resurgence of Marxist/Socialist ideas should not be surprising. Despite the fall of Communist regimes around the world, the essential ideas of Marxism/Socialism remained, and still remain, largely untouched and unchallenged. These ideas pertain to the relationship between capitalists and wage earners, and they are accepted by the great majority of people in the United States and throughout the world.

MARXISM/SOCIALISM, A SOCIOPATHIC PHILOSOPHY

They are accepted not as being descriptive of the way conditions actually are in the United States or in any other advanced country of the present day, but as descriptive of the way conditions *would be* in the absence of major government intervention. And they are accepted as both descriptive and explanatory of the way conditions were in the nineteenth century.

Thus, people believe that in the absence of government intervention in the form of pro-union, minimum-wage, maximum-hours, and child-labor legislation, and laws regulating working conditions, the capitalists, in their greedy pursuit of profits, would drive wages down to, or even below, minimum physical subsistence, lengthen the hours of work to the maximum possible, force small children to work in factories and mines, and make working conditions unbearable for all. All that allegedly stands in the way of this nightmare-world ready to be unleashed by the unrestricted operation of capitalism and the profit motive is legislation inspired by Marxism/Socialism. This view of things appears to be held, and to have been held for more than a century, by virtually all Democrats and perhaps half or more of the Republicans.

The refutation of these and many other major errors about the nature of capitalism, along with a demonstration of the destructive and totalitarian nature of socialism, is the subject of this essay. To connect these remarks to the title of my essay, let me say that Marxism/Socialism is a philosophy conceived in gross error and ignorance about the nature of capitalism, above all about the nature of the relationship between capitalists, profits, and wages. Socialism is little more than a violent rejection of capitalism, based on this combination of errors and ignorance, and which, once having managed to destroy capitalism, results in economic chaos, enslavement, terror, and mass murder. Socialism and its consequences can be likened to the assault of a barbarian tribe become enraged at the relative prosperity of a civilized land. After destroying the fields, the livestock, the roads, and the aqueducts of the civilized land, it finds itself with nothing but a few remaining scraps over which its members kill one another. That is the essential situation of today's socialist barbarians, inspired by Marx to hate capitalists and the civilization that they have built.

What the socialist barbarians destroy is private ownership of the means of production, the profit motive, private saving and capital accumulation, competition, and the price system. In destroying them, these barbarians have no idea that in doing so they are destroying the foundations of material civilization, in which they have shared and could continue to share. It is the purpose of this essay to teach those of them that both know how to read and have not yet reached the point of burning the writings they fear, the actual nature of capitalism and of Marxism/Socialism, in the hope that they will then become defenders, rather than destroyers, of capitalist civilization.

PART I. THE GIST OF MARXISM/SOCIALISM AND ITS REFUTATION

I. 1. The Essential Nature of Socialism: The Need for Armed Robbery to Establish It

First of all, it must be realized that there is no such thing as socialism without government ownership of the means of production. That is the essential, defining characteristic of socialism. Second, there is only one way to establish socialism. And that is by means of *armed robbery on a massive scale*. Even a democratically elected socialist government would have to send armed men out through the country to seize the means of production. For there is no other way that it could obtain ownership of them. (The fact that it was democratically elected would be of as little significance as the fact that, compared with its victims, a lynch mob typically constitutes an overwhelming majority.) Unlike the case of nationalizing an isolated industry here and there, in which the government can pay meaningful compensation to the owners, by means of raising taxes on the rest of the economic system, the government has no way to compensate the owners of means of production as a class, for there is no source of wealth outside the economic system. Furthermore, insofar as socialists believe that capitalists are thieves living off profits stolen from the wage earners, they do not want to compensate the capitalists, even if they could.

In these circumstances of total loss, many capitalists will resist the theft of their property. They will forcibly defend what is theirs.

At this point, a newly installed socialist government is put in the position of a would-be street robber who must make a fundamental decision. If the street robber wants to take someone's wallet, it is not enough for him to approach his victim and say something like, "Please, Sir, give me your wallet." The intended victim may give him a punch in the nose instead. If the robber really wants the wallet, he needs to come with a gun, to threaten the victim's life if he does not turn over his wallet. That is what the socialist state must do if it wants the capitalists' property. It must come with enough force to overcome the armed resistance of its victims, which entails its' committing murder on a large scale, very possibly on the scale entailed in the civil war it may provoke.

What this means is that to establish socialism, what is required are *the communists!* The communists are armed robbers prepared to commit murder. They are the true champions of socialism. They alone can openly establish it.[3]

I. 2. The Social Democrats Should Stop Calling Themselves Socialists

The need to use armed force to establish socialism has created a major split in the socialist movement. The split is between the communists, who are the true socialists, and the social democrats. The social democrats continue to talk about establishing socialism and continue to describe themselves as socialists, but they have managed to retain enough moral sense to want to avoid mass bloodshed. As a result, they effectively abandon socialism as their actual goal when they have the opportunity to achieve it.

When they come to power, the social democrats retain capitalism as the economic system, though they may further hamper its operation with additional taxes and regulations. Sweden, Norway, France, et al. are capitalist countries, not socialist countries,[4] despite the fact that they are typically described as socialist and their ruling parties are typically known as socialist parties. The truth is that the means of production in these countries are privately owned to more or less the same extent as they are in the United States, and they are employed by their owners in order "to make profits and avoid losses," as von Mises put it. This is not socialism, but capitalism, even if badly hampered capitalism.

Consistent with the laws of logic, the social democrats need to stop calling themselves socialists and to insist that no one else call them socialists. This is because the word "socialist" means "one who advocates socialism." Inasmuch as socialism means government ownership of the means of production, the word "socialist" logically implies that one is an advocate of government ownership of the means of production, which, in the real world of choosing and acting, the social democrats—to their credit—have repeatedly shown that they are not.

Unless and until the social democrats abandon the use of the word "socialist" to describe themselves, they are in the position of giving aid and comfort to a philosophy and a system of government that is responsible for untold human misery and the deaths of tens of millions of innocent people. There is nothing that can justify this.

I. 3. The Marxists/Socialists' Rationalization for the Armed Robbery Needed to Establish Socialism: Alleged "Exploitation" and "Wage Slavery" under Capitalism

As I have indicated, the Marxists/Socialists have a rationalization for their desire to steal the means of production from the capitalists, and to murder the capitalists. They claim that the capitalists are thieves—that they they steal their profits from the wage earners through the imposition of "wage slavery" and "exploitation," and that the capital the capitalists have saved up and accumulated out of those profits over the generations is thus property taken from the wage earners in the first place. The Marxists/Socialists, who allegedly act on behalf of the wage earners, in now stealing the means of production from the capitalists are allegedly merely stealing them back— they are guilty of nothing more than "the expropriation of the expropriators," to use a favorite expression of the Marxists/Socialists. Here is what *The Great Soviet Encyclopedia* (1979) has to say on the subject:

> The expropriation of the expropriators is lawful, since the sizable property of the exploiting class was accumulated by robbing and mercilessly exploiting the working masses. Therefore, depriving the exploiters of their property is a legitimate and justified act. The working people thereby regain the wealth that they created, that is rightfully theirs, and that was taken from them by force.[5]

This Marxist/Socialist rationalization for theft and murder omits the fact that but for the alleged thievery of the capitalists, there would be nothing for the Marxists/Socialists to steal. Unlike real-life thieves who typically consume their loot in buying drugs, alcohol, and the services of loose women, the alleged capitalist thieves save and invest their alleged loot. They accumulate capital in the form of materials, tools, machines, buildings, and all kinds of infrastructure, as well as use a substantial portion of it to pay wages. Thus, without them and without their alleged thievery, there would be nothing for the Marxists/Socialists to steal.

Further, while the capitalists accumulate capital, their alleged victims do not. If the capitalists' alleged victims did accumulate capital out of their earnings, as the capitalists do, the Marxists/Socialists would no longer describe them as victims but as capitalist exploiters. According to Marxism/Socialism, in order not to be a capitalist exploiter and thief, one must not accumulate capital, for if one does, one is then a capitalist and therefore an exploiter and thief. So the claim that the theft of the capitalists' wealth qualifies as a return of wealth to the wage earners, who did not accumulate any part of it and never had any of it, is simply an absurdity. Furthermore, what the capitalists allegedly took from the wage earners, according to the Marxist/Socialists was never any actual, tangible property, but *labor* for which they allegedly did not pay. And the alleged proof of this, according to the Marxists/Socialists, is that *anything whatever* that the capitalists receive in the process of production represents labor for which they allegedly do not pay. This is because, according to the Marxists/Socialists, the entire value added in the productive process belongs by right to the wage earners and thus anything whatever that the capitalists obtain is an unjust deduction—a theft—of part of what is naturally and rightfully wages.

As just indicated, the Marxists/Socialists believe that the essential feature of capitalism is the "exploitation" of the labor of wage earners. The capitalists allegedly get their profits by stealing as much as possible from what naturally and rightfully belongs to the wage earners as wages. Indeed, they allegedly gain in just the same way that a slave owner gains. Hence, the expression "wage slaves," which implies that the workers employed by capitalists are in fact slaves and only superficially appear to be free. Yes, "freedom is slavery," say the Marxists/Socialists.[6]

A slave owner gains by virtue of the fact that a slave is able to accomplish more in a day or a week than is required to keep him alive. The master appropriates the difference—the surplus, as the Marxists call it. And that, say the

Marxists/Socialists is just what the capitalists do. The capitalists pay wages just sufficient to provide minimum subsistence, and compel the workers to work as much as possible beyond the hours required to produce that minimum, and thus to bring in for the capitalists as much money as possible beyond the sum of money required to purchase that minimum. All the money that the wage earners bring in for the capitalists over and above what is required for them to purchase minimum subsistence is allegedly pocketed by the capitalists as profit or "surplus-value," to employ Marxist jargon. (Interest, and any other income that is not a wage or a salary, is included under the heading of profit.)

This is the gist of the Marxian exploitation theory. Marx, however, takes over 800 pages to present it.[7] I will turn to the details of Marx's presentation in terms of the labor theory of value in Part II of this essay, so that readers can appreciate the extent of his ignorance, intellectual dishonesty, and sociopathy.

I. 4. The Essential Difference between Free Labor and Slave Labor that Marxism/Socialism Ignores

Meanwhile, it is of the utmost importance to point out that in describing the wage earners of capitalism as slaves, the Marxists/Socialists omit an essential difference. A slave is kept at his work by means of physical force, e.g., chains, whips, and guns. In sharpest contrast, the free worker of capitalism, especially one who would otherwise starve to death if he did not have a job, is not kept at his work by means of force. On the contrary, it would take force to *keep him from his work*. The wages that a capitalist employer offers are a positive that enable the worker to live and which he is prepared to make every effort to earn. The capitalist employer stands in service to the worker's life. In contrast, the beating that a slave owner offers is a negative that impairs the worker's life.

In strict Marxist/Socialist fashion, John Kenneth Galbraith, a prominent writer of the last century, who was widely applauded in his time, attempts to obliterate this distinction, and thus justify the description of wage earners under capitalism as slaves. He writes:

> The worker in a Calcutta jute mill who loses his job—like his American counterpart during the Great Depression—has no high prospect of ever finding another. He has no savings. Nor does he have unemployment insurance. The alternative to his present employment, accordingly, is slow but definite starvation. So though nominally a free worker, he is compelled. The fate of a defecting southern slave before the Civil War or a serf before Alexander II was not appreciably more painful. The choice between hunger and flogging may well be a matter of taste.[8]

I quote Galbraith's concluding sentence again: "The choice between hunger and flogging may well be a matter of taste." Thus, according to Galbraith, pain is pain, irrespective of whether it's caused by the lack of food or by a flogging, and it makes no difference whether there is a capitalist, whose payment of wages prevents the pain of hunger, or a slave owner, whose whip imposes the pain of a flogging. Pain, capitalist, slave owner—it's all the same. The conclusion to be drawn from Galbraith's, and all similar such passages by countless other writers, is that the capitalists are the same as slave owners and deserve to be shot. What is this if not a mentality of the stupid and vicious, of morons and murderers? A mentality that sees no difference between the use of physical force to *make* someone work and a need for physical force to *stop* someone from working. A mentality that treats as the same, two cases in which a worker works to avoid pain, neglecting that in the one case the pain is caused by a master and in the other, caused by nature and prevented by a capitalist. A mentality, in other words, that sees no difference between slavery and freedom, and thus can claim justification for Marxists/Socialists robbing and murdering capitalists on the grounds that the free workers of the capitalists are their slaves.

This is how the Marxists/Socialists attempt to put over their Orwellian claim that "freedom is slavery." Given the profoundly evil nature of the claim, which simultaneously devalues freedom and makes slavery appear as no worse than freedom, this gross error could also be classified as a major manifestation of sociopathy on the part of Marxism/Socialism.

I. 5. Adam Smith as the Father of the Marxian Exploitation Theory

What enables Marx to believe that the conditions of a wage earner under capitalism are essentially the same as those of a slave under outright slavery, is, first or all, a set of three gross errors propounded by no less than Adam Smith, the man who is generally regarded as the father of capitalism. The first of these errors is *the confusion of labor with wage earning*, as though to perform labor were synonymous with wage earning. The second error is drawing the inference that in a world in which there are no businessmen or capitalists, but only manual workers, the income of these workers is wages. The third error is that, on the basis of these errors, *profit appears as an income that was originally wages, and naturally and rightfully still is wages, but is now taken from the wage earners to constitute the profits of their employers.*

These errors are clearly expressed in the following passages from *The Wealth of Nations*:

> The produce of labour constitutes the natural recompence or wages of labour.
>
> In that original state of things, which precedes both the appropriation of land and the accumulation of stock [capital], the whole produce of labour belongs to the labourer. He has neither landlord nor master to share with him.
>
> Had this state continued, the wages of labour would have augmented with all those improvements in its productive powers, to which the division of labour gives occasion....
>
> The produce of almost all other labour is liable to the like deduction of profit. In all arts and manufactures the greater part of the workmen stand in need of a master to advance them the materials of their work, and their wages and maintenance till it be compleated. He shares in the produce of their labour, or in the value which it adds to the materials on which it is bestowed; and in this share consists his profit.[9]

Adam Smith's notion that profits are a deduction from wages contradicts everyday experience. But it has gone unchallenged for almost two and a half centuries. In normal, everyday business and accounting practice, profits are not a deduction from anything. On the contrary, they are *the result of deductions*. They are what remains after the deduction of wages and all other costs from sales revenues. Nevertheless, Marx makes Smith's gross error—Smith's treatment of the result of deductions as though *it* were a deduction—the starting point of his exposition of his world-famous exploitation theory. The exploitation theory begins with Smith's notion that profits are a deduction from wages and then goes on to claim that the size of the deduction is limited only by the workers' need for enough wages to keep themselves alive.

We need to start with the fact that capitalists do not deduct profits from wages, do not steal profits from wage earners. Contrary to Smith and Marx, the economic world did not begin in a condition in which all income was wages and then, only later, when capitalists appeared on the scene, did the phenomenon of profit emerge—as a deduction from what was originally all wages. Indeed, Marx himself, had he looked, was in a position easily to realize this.

I. 6. Marx's "Simple Circulation" and "Capitalistic Circulation"

Marx begins his analysis of the alleged exploitation of labor under capitalism with a distinction between the fundamental economic character of the ages that preceded capitalism and the fundamental economic character of capitalism. The distinction he makes is between two sorts of the circulation of money from hand to hand. The one sort, he calls "simple circulation." It supposedly characterized economic conditions prior to capitalism. ("Simple circulation," it should be noted, is actually the same state of affairs that Adam Smith described in *The Wealth of Nations* as "the original state of things.")

Under simple circulation, manual workers produce commodities, designated by "C," sell them for money, designated by "M," and then use the money earned to buy other commodities, also designated by "C." Thus, simple circulation is the sequence C-M-C. Under simple circulation, there is allegedly no exploitation of labor. The workers—the wage earners—receive the full proceeds brought in by the sale of their products. These sales proceeds are viewed as indistinguishable from wage payments, as though they were in fact wage payments. This is because, following the practice of Adam Smith, all income due to the performance of labor is assumed to be wages. To say it once more, in simple circulation all income earned in producing commodities for sale is regarded as wages. Smith provides the clearest possible example of this view when he writes, "In some parts of Scotland a few poor people make a trade of gathering, along the sea-shore, those little variegated stones commonly known by the name of Scotch Pebbles. The price which is paid to them by the stone cutter is altogether the wages of their labour; neither rent nor profit make any part of it."[10]

The exploitation of labor begins, according to Marx, only with the coming of capitalists and "capitalistic circulation."[11] Here the starting point is an outlay of money by the capitalists to pay wages and buy previously produced commodities in such forms as materials and tools and, ultimately, also machines and factory buildings. These outlays of money are for the purpose of producing commodities that are to be sold in the market, hopefully, in the view of the capitalist, for a larger sum of money than he has expended in producing them. Thus, capitalistic circulation is represented by the sequence M-C-M or, more precisely, by the sequence M-C-M', with M' used to represent the second M as being larger than the first and thus the sequence as a whole as showing a profit.[12]

I. 7. Profits, Not Wages, as the Original and Primary form of Labor Income

Now the position of Smith and Marx is utterly absurd. The obvious fact is that in simple circulation there are *no wages* paid in production. Manual workers, true enough, are the only recipients of income, but the money they earn is *not* wages. It is *sales revenues*. They are producing and selling their products, not their labor. A wage is money paid in exchange for the performance of labor. What is paid in exchange for a product of labor is a sales revenue, not a wage. Thus, what is paid for Smith's "Scotch Pebbles" or any other good or product, is sales revenues, not wages. In the words of John Stuart Mill:

> Demand for commodities is not demand for labour....This theorem, that to purchase produce is not to employ labour; that the demand for labour is constituted by the wages which precede the production, and not by the demand which may exist for the commodities resulting from the production; is a proposition which greatly needs all the illustration it can receive.[13]

Let me proceed immediately to give Mill's proposition some of its much needed illustration.

Thus, one simple proof of Mill's proposition is that if one did buy the labor that produces a product, one would *not* have to buy that product, because one would already own it, in which case having to buy it would be a form of swindle. For example, if I employ a housekeeper, pay her wages and give her money to buy groceries, and she then cooks me a dinner, I am not presented with a check for the dinner, because having bought the means necessary to its production, I already own that dinner and therefore do not have to buy it. If in these circumstances I were somehow made to pay a check for the dinner, I would be the victim of a crime. By the same token, when I go to a restaurant and legitimately have to pay the check for my dinner, it is because I have *not* bought the labor and materials, etc., necessary to its production. In other words, *if you buy the output, it is because you have not bought the inputs.* If you had bought the inputs, you would not be buying the output, because you would already own it. Thus the buyer of a commodity does not buy the labor that produced that commodity. He does not pay wages but product sales revenues.

Furthermore, to claim that in buying a product one buys the labor and/or anything else necessary to the production of that product, such as the materials or equipment required in its production, entails the contradiction of claiming that one is simultaneously buying *not* for the purpose of selling and buying *for* the purpose of selling. For example, the purchase of a loaf of bread by a consumer is *not* for the purpose of making subsequent sales. However, the expenditure for the flour and the labor of a baker necessary to the production of that loaf of bread *is* for the purpose of making subsequent sales. Thus, if somehow in buying the loaf of bread one were buying the flour and labor of a baker necessary to its production, one would simultaneously, in the very same act, be not buying for the purpose of subsequently selling and buying for the purpose of subsequently selling.

Finally, and most importantly, as we shall see, demand for commodities is not only not demand for labor but regularly and consistently *exceeds* the demand for labor and that *this fact is the main source of profit in the economic system.* Profit is the excess of sales revenues over costs. Since demand (expenditure) for capital goods appears equally both in sales revenues and in costs, it is precisely the excess of demand for consumers' goods over the capitalists' demand for labor that is the source of profit in the economic system.[14]

As soon as one joins with Mill in realizing that the purchase of a commodity is not a purchase of the labor that produced it, a fatal problem arises for the whole philosophy of Marxism/Socialism. And that is, that not only do the workers under simple circulation earn sales revenues rather than wages, but they also have *zero costs of production* to deduct from those sales revenues, since, as yet, no one has expended any money for the purpose of bringing in sales revenues. Costs of production are nothing but the reflection of prior outlays of money for the purpose of bringing in sales revenues and thereby, to the extent that the sales revenues exceed the outlays, earn a profit. But such outlays are simply not present under simple circulation. Smith and Marx have both told us so. They exist only under capitalistic circulation.

And thus we reach what will understandably appear to many as an amazing conclusion: not only is the money earned by the workers under simple circulation sales revenues rather than wages, but also it is *profit*. The entire sales proceeds earned by the workers under simple circulation are profit, because, in the absence of buying for the sake of selling, there are no costs to deduct from the sales revenues, and thus the entire sales revenues turn out to be profit: M`-0=M`.

This conclusion means that *profit,* not wages, *is the original, primary form of labor income*. It also means that capitalists are not responsible for the existence of the phenomenon of profit, since it exists prior to their existence.

I. 8. Capitalists Responsible for Wages, Costs, and Reduction of Profits

A further conclusion follows. Namely, that what capitalists are responsible for is not only not the phenomenon of profit but rather the phenomena of *wages, expenditure for capital goods, and costs of production*. Capitalists are responsible for the first M in capitalistic circulation. That M represents the wages paid in production plus the expenditure for capital goods, and shows up as costs of production to be deducted from sales revenues.

It also follows that by virtue of creating the phenomenon of costs of production, i.e., the costs that show up in business income statements, the activity of the capitalists serves to *reduce the proportion of sales revenues that is profit.* Capitalists do not create profit and subtract it from wages. On the contrary, they create wages and the other costs which are subtracted from sales revenues, and thus the capitalists reduce the proportion of sales revenues that is profit. Of course, in creating wages and costs, capitalists not only reduce the proportion of sales revenues that is profit, but they also increase the proportion of sales revenues that equals wages, adding positive amounts to an initial amount of zero, and at the same time correspondingly increasing the ratio of wages to profits. Thus, capitalists create wages and reduce profits in terms of their respective size relative to sales revenues.

It follows that capitalists do not impoverish wage earners, but make it possible for people to *be* wage earners. For, as I have shown, they are responsible not for the phenomenon of profit, but for the phenomenon of wages. They are responsible for the very existence of wages in the production of products for sale.

Without other people existing as capitalists, the only way in which one could survive in connection with the production and sale of products would be by means of producing and selling one's own products, namely, as a profit earner. But to produce and sell one's own products, one would have to produce or have inherited one's own tools and materials. Relatively few people could survive in this way. The existence of capitalists makes it possible for people to live by selling their labor rather than attempting to sell the products of their labor. Thus, between wage earners and capitalists there is in fact the closest possible *harmony of interests*, for capitalists create wages and the ability of people to survive and prosper as wage earners.[15]

Historical confirmation for the theory I am propounding can be found in F. A. Hayek's Introduction to *Capitalism and the Historians*. There we find such statements as: "The actual history of the connection between capitalism and the rise of the proletariat is almost the exact opposite of that which these theories of the expropriation of the masses suggest.… The proletariat which capitalism can be said to have 'created' was thus not a proportion of the population which would have existed without it and which it degraded to a lower level; it was an additional population which was enabled to grow up by the new opportunities for employment which capitalism provided."[16]

A simple application of Marx's formula for capitalistic circulation brings all this out. All we need do is take the first M of the sequence and divide it by the second M of the sequence. I call the resulting mathematical expression, M/M′, the *economic degree of capitalism*. Simple circulation represents a zero economic degree of capitalism. It is expressed as 0/M′. The more economically capitalistic the economic system is, the higher are wage payments relative to sales revenues and the higher is the expenditure for capital goods relative to sales revenues. Putting aside the negative effects of confiscatory taxation and government deficit spending, both of which deprive capitalists of funds they would otherwise spend in buying labor and capital goods, today's economic degree of capitalism might be on the order of .9 or .95, or even higher. Profits would then be equivalent perhaps to less than a mere 5 or 10 percent of business sales revenues, wages equivalent to perhaps 40 or 45 percent, or even more, and purchases of capital goods equivalent to the remaining 50 percent or more of business sales revenues.

Thus, so far from the actual relationship between capitalists and wage earners being one of class warfare, as the Marxists/Socialists claim, it is one of *class harmony*. The only warfare that exists here is a warfare waged by the Marxists/Socialists on the basis of their misidentification of profits as wages and their belief that the capitalists, who create wages and reduce profits, instead create profits and reduce wages.

I. 9. Profits Still an Income Earned by the Labor of Capitalists

Before developing further the implications of the economic degree of capitalism for the standard of living of the average wage earner, it is necessary to develop somewhat further the implications of the fact that profits are an income earned by the performance of labor by their recipients, indeed, are the original, primary form of labor income. Clearly this is the case under simple circulation. It is no less the case under capitalistic circulation, where profits continue to be the income of the sellers of products. These workers, now businessmen and capitalists, continue to earn profits and continue to do so by virtue of their performance of labor.

However, in the conditions of "capitalistic circulation" and its high degree of division of labor,[17] the labor of those who sell their products comes, in most cases, to be mainly, indeed, overwhelmingly of an intellectual character—a labor of thinking, planning, and decision making—rather than manual labor. This fact is responsible for creating a close connection between the amount of profit that is earned and the size of the businessman's or capitalist's capital. This is because the larger is the businessman's or capitalist's capital, the larger is the scale on which he can implement his ideas and plans. For the greater is his capital, the larger is the number of helpers he can employ and the better he can equip them and provide them with all other necessary means of production, such as materials and components, and, of course, the physical structures in which they work. Thus, a businessman or capitalist with $100 million of capital can implement his ideas and plans on ten times the scale of a businessman or capitalist with only $10 million of capital. As a result, it should not be surprising that he may earn ten times the profit even though the quantity of his labor of thinking, planning, and decision making may be the same or nearly the same in both cases.

The variation of profits with the amount of capital invested, rather than simply the physical quantity of labor performed, led Adam Smith to make the mistake of believing that profits therefore could not be attributed to any performance of labor by businessmen or capitalists but were somehow the result just of the employment of capitals of different size.[18] Smith did not realize that the same reasoning could be used to deny that manual labor produces anything more than what can be produced by people using nothing but their bare hands.

Consider. The same quantity of physical labor produces radically different results, depending on the magnitude and potency of the means of production it employs. A worker digging with only his bare hands is able to move only a very small amount of earth in any given time. If he could use a shovel, he would be able to move far more earth in the same period of time. And if he were able to use a steam shovel, he would be able to move an amount of earth much larger still. Nevertheless, at every point, no matter what its size, the hole that is dug is always the product of labor. In the first case, a worker digs only a very small hole; in the second, a much larger hole; in the third, a vastly still larger hole. But in all three cases, it is still the worker who digs the hole. Every product is the product of human labor.

How do these cases differ fundamentally from the case of a capitalist with $100 million of capital earning ten times the profit as a capitalist with only $10 million of capital, and a capitalist with $1 billion of capital earning ten times the profit of the capitalist with $100 million of capital? They don't. The two sets of cases are the same.

In all cases, products are products of human labor. The reason that they are products of human labor is that it is human labor that supplies the guiding and directing intelligence in production. A manual worker directs his hands to dig a hole; he directs the shovel in digging a larger hole; he directs the steam shovel in digging a still larger hole. In all cases, the hole is the product of his guiding and directing intelligence.

Now in the economic system businessmen and capitalists supply guiding and directing intelligence in production at a higher level than do wage earners. They employ and equip the wage earners to achieve the results at which they, the businessmen and capitalists, are aiming. The wage earners are their helpers in carrying out their plans and thus in achieving their goals. Thus, a businessman or capitalist buys a steam shovel and hires a worker to operate it. He tells the worker where to dig a hole and how large a hole to dig. He, the businessman or capitalist is the party who makes the decision to have the hole dug, assembles all the means necessary to accomplish it, gives the order to dig it, and makes sure that it is dug. In this way, in causing the hole to be dug, he is the party in the productive process who is fundamentally responsible for the digging of the hole. The hole is *his* product. The wage earner in the case is a helper in producing what is the businessman's or capitalist's product.

Attributing results to those who supply the guiding and directing intelligence at the highest level is the common practice outside the realm of material production. Thus, history teaches such things as that Columbus discovered America and Napoleon won the battle of Austerlitz. The newspapers write of the President's foreign policy. Why isn't the discovery of America attributed to the various crew members on Columbus's ships, the victory at Austerlitz to the various soldiers in Napoleon's army, and our country's foreign policy to the various State Department employees? All of these people certainly played, or play, a role. The reason is that it was these three parties that supplied, or supply, the guiding and directing intelligence at the highest level in these cases. It was Columbus who had the vision that the earth was round and that sailing far enough west would necessarily bring one to the east and who did not stop until his expedition finally found landfall. It was Napoleon who supplied the basic strategy of the French at Austerlitz. It is the President who makes the basic decisions underlying our foreign policy.

Now by the same standard of attribution as is normally followed in history books and elsewhere, the products of the old Ford Motor Company must be attributed to Henry Ford and those of the old Standard Oil Company to John D. Rockefeller. The same applies to such modern-day business giants as Jobs, Gates, and Bezos and to all the lesser known figures who are represented only by the names of their companies. The products are theirs, not the men on the assembly lines. The men on the assembly lines, the wage earners of all descriptions, are the "help." They are the helpers of the businessmen and capitalists in producing their, the businessmen's and capitalists', products.

Once it is realized that the products of firms are fundamentally products of the labor of businessmen and capitalists, the slogan "labor's right to the whole produce" turns out to be a demand which is already met under capitalism, every minute of every day, i.e., whenever businessmen and capitalists, or the firms under whose names they do business, are paid for *their* products.

It is remarkable that Marxism/Socialism is not only totally unaware of the productive role of businessmen and capitalists and claims their products for the wage earners, but also complains that the wage earners under capitalism are "alienated" from their work and have no real sense of connection with it, as though products could be produced under such conditions, i.e., in the absence of anyone appreciating the value of the products and understanding the interconnections of all the various steps in their production and seeing to it that the individual steps all fit together. Thus, these alleged "alienated" victims of the capitalists not only never had any accumulated capital to steal, as I explained earlier, they also do not even have the ability by themselves to produce anything that would be worth stealing.[19] It is the capitalists who are the fundamental, primary producers, not them.

I. 10. Passive Capitalists

There are many capitalists, such as most small stock or bond holders, minor children with stock or bond holdings large or small, and many widows, who play no role in the operations of the firms in which their capital is invested. These people, it could be argued are passive capitalists, dependent for their incomes on the labor of others.

The first thing to realize about such cases is that if they did constitute an exploitation of labor, it would not be the labor of the wage earners that was being exploited, but the labor of the businessmen and capitalists that produced the incomes of the passive capitalists. If there were an exploitation of labor here, it would be a case of widows and orphans exploiting the labor of Ford and Rockefeller.

Actually, however, there is no exploitation of labor present. The businessmen and capitalists who pay the dividends and interest of the passive capitalists, gain in the process. Their employment of the capitals of the passive capitalists typically enables them to earn profits greater than the dividends or interest that they pay.

Finally, it is not the case that the dividends and interest of stock and bondholders who play no active role in the running of the firms in which their capital is invested are by any means necessarily unearned. There is no limit to the thought and research that can be put into stock or bond purchases. And to the extent that investors put in thought and do research on their investments, their incomes must be judged to be earned.

I. 11. The Irrelevance of "Worker Need" and "Employer Greed" in the Determination of Wages[20]

While Adam Smith originated the doctrine that profits are a deduction from what is naturally and rightfully wages, Marx carried that doctrine to its ultimate limit, in the claim that the greed of the capitalists drives them to deduct so much from what rightfully belongs to the wage earners that the latter are left only with minimum subsistence. This is Marx's version of the so-called "iron law of wages." Its essential claim is that employers have the power arbitrarily to set wages at minimum subsistence, irrespective of the state of capital accumulation, technology, and the productivity of labor.[21]

What makes Marx's doctrine of the alleged arbitrary power of employers over wages appear plausible is that there are two obvious facts which do not actually support it but which appear to support it. These facts can be described as "worker need" and "employer greed."

The average worker must work in order to live, and he must find work fairly quickly, because his savings cannot sustain him for long. And if necessary—if he had no alternative—he would be willing to work for as little as minimum physical subsistence. At the same time, self-interest makes employers, like any other buyers, prefer to pay less rather than more—to pay lower wages rather than higher wages. People put these two facts together and conclude that if employers were free, wages would be driven down by the force of the employers' self-interest—as though by a giant plunger pushing down in an empty cylinder—and that no resistance to the fall in wages would be encountered until the point of minimum subsistence was reached. At that point, it is held, workers would refuse to work because starvation without the strain of labor would be preferable to starvation with the strain of labor. Thus, if the capitalist is to find workers, he must pay them at least minimum subsistence and no less.

What must be realized is that while it is true that workers would be willing to work for minimum subsistence if necessary and that self-interest makes employers prefer to pay less rather than more, both of these facts are *irrelevant* to the wages the workers actually have to accept in the labor market.

Let us start with "worker need." To understand why a worker's willingness to work for subsistence if necessary is irrelevant to the wages he actually has to work for, consider the case of the owner of a late-model car who decides to accept a job offer, and to live, in the heart of New York City. If this car owner cannot afford several hundred dollars a month to pay the cost of keeping his car in a garage, and if he cannot devote several prime working hours every week to driving around, hunting for places to park his car on the street, he will be willing, if he can find no better offer, to give his car away for free—indeed, to pay someone to come and take it off his hands. Yet the fact that he is willing to do this is absolutely irrelevant to the price he actually must accept for his car. That price is determined on the basis of the utility and scarcity of used cars—by the demand for and supply of such cars. Indeed, so long as the number of used cars offered for sale remained the same, and the demand for used cars remained the same, it would not matter even if every seller of such a car were willing to give his car away for free, or willing even to pay to have it taken off his hands. None of them would have to accept a zero or negative price or any price that is significantly different from the price he presently can receive.

This point is illustrated in terms of the simple supply and demand diagram presented in Figure 1. On the vertical axis, I depict the price of used cars, designated by P. On the horizontal axis, I depict the quantity of used cars, designated by Q, that sellers are prepared to sell and the buyers to buy at any given price. The willingness of sellers to sell some definite, given quantity of used cars at any price from zero on up (or, indeed, from less than zero by the cost of having the cars taken off their hands) is depicted by a vertical line drawn through that quantity. The vertical line SS denotes the fact that sellers are willing to sell the

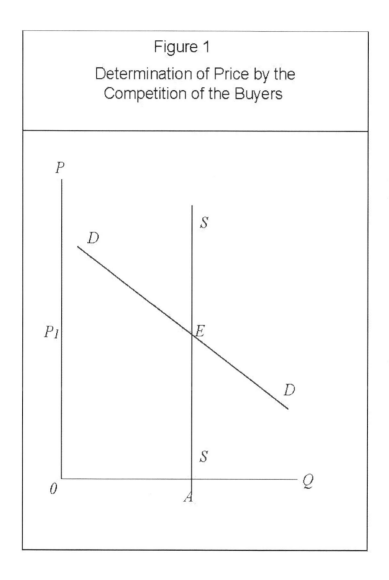

specific quantity A of used cars at any price from something less than zero on up to as much as they can get for their cars.

The fact that the sellers are willing to sell for zero or a negative price has nothing whatever to do with the actual price they receive, which in this case is the very positive price P_1. The actual price they receive in a case of this kind is determined by the limitation of the supply of used cars, together with the demand for used cars. In Figure 1, it is determined at point E, which represents the intersection of the vertical supply line with the downward sloping demand line.[22]

The price that corresponds to that juncture of supply and demand is P_1. The fact that the sellers are all willing if necessary to accept a price less than P_1 is, as I say, simply irrelevant to the price they actually must accept. The price the sellers receive in a case of this kind is not determined by the terms on which they are willing to sell. Rather, it is determined by the competition of the buyers for the limited supply offered for sale. This, of course, is the kind of case that the great Austrian-school economist Böhm-Bawerk had in mind when he declared that "price is actually limited and determined by the valuations on the part of the buyers exclusively."[23]

Essentially the same diagram, Figure 2, depicts the case of labor. Instead of showing price on the vertical axis, I show wages, designated by W. Instead of the supply line being vertical to the point of the sellers being willing to pay to have their good taken off their their hands, I assume that no supply whatever is offered below the point of "minimum subsistence," M. This is depicted by a horizontal line drawn from M and parallel to the horizontal axis. Thus, the supply "curve" in this case has a horizontal portion at "minimum

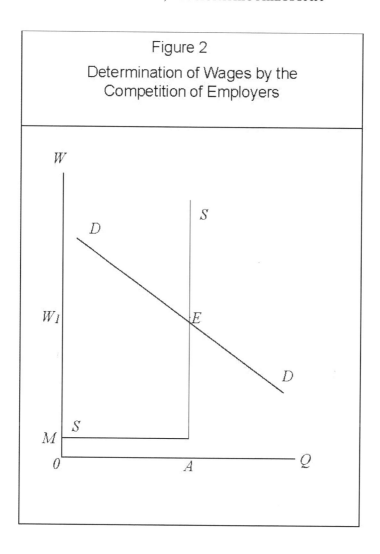

Figure 2
Determination of Wages by the Competition of Employers

subsistence" before becoming vertical. These are the only differences between Figures 1 and 2.

Figure 2 makes clear that the fact that the workers are willing to work for as little as minimum subsistence is no more relevant to the wages they actually have to accept than was the fact in the previous example that the sellers of used cars were willing to give them away for free or pay to have them taken off their hands. For even though the workers are willing to work for as little as minimum subsistence, the wage they actually obtain in the conditions of the market is the incomparably higher wage W_1, which is shown by the intersection—once again at point E—of the demand for labor with the limited supply of labor denoted by point A on the horizontal axis. Exactly like the value of used cars, or anything else that exists in a given, limited supply, the value of labor is determined on a foundation of its utility and scarcity, by demand and supply—more specifically, by the competition of buyers for the limited supply—not by any form of cost of production, least of all by any "cost of production of labor."

It also quickly becomes clear that "employer greed" is fully as irrelevant to the determination of wage rates as "worker need." This becomes apparent as soon as the case of the art auction is considered that I originally presented in *Capitalism*[24] in order to demonstrate the actual self-interest of buyers. There I assumed that there are two people at an art auction, both of whom want the same painting. One of these people, let us now call him Mr. Smith, is willing and able to bid as high as $2,000 for the painting. The other, let us now call him Mr. Jones, is willing and able to go no higher than $1,000. Of course, Mr. Smith does not want to spend $2,000 for the painting. This figure is merely the limit of how high he will go if he has to. He would much prefer to obtain the painting for only $200, or better still, for only $20, or, best of all, for nothing at all. What we must consider here is precisely how low a bid Mr. Smith's rational self-interest allows him to persist in. Would it, for example, actually be to Mr. Smith's self-interest to persist in a bid of only $20, or $200?

It should be obvious that the answer to this question is decidedly no! This is because if Mr. Smith persists in such a low bid, the effect will be that he loses the painting to Mr. Jones, who is willing and able to bid more than $20 and more than $200. In fact, in the conditions of this case, Mr. Smith must lose the painting to the higher bidding of Mr. Jones, if he persists in bidding any sum under $1,000! If Mr. Smith is to obtain the painting, the conditions of the case require him to bid more than $1,000, because that is the sum required to exceed the maximum potential bid of Mr. Jones.

This case contains the fundamental principle that names the actual self-interest of buyers. That principle is that a buyer rationally desires to pay not the lowest price he would like or can imagine, but the lowest price that is simultaneously too high for any other potential buyer of the good, who would otherwise obtain the good in his place. Here that minimum price is $1,001.

This identical principle, of course, applies to the determination of wage rates. The only difference between the labor market and the auction of a painting is the number of units involved. Instead of one painting with two potential buyers for it, there are many millions of workers who must sell their services, together with potential employers of all those workers and of untold millions more workers. This is because just as in the example of the art auction, the essential fact that is present in the labor market is that the potential quantity demanded exceeds the supply available. The potential quantity of labor demanded always far exceeds the quantity of labor that the workers are able, let alone willing, to perform.

For labor, it should be realized, is scarce. It is the most fundamentally useful and scarce thing in the economic system: virtually everything else that is useful is its product and is limited in supply only by virtue of our lack of ability or willingness to expend more labor to produce a larger quantity of it. (This, of course, includes raw materials, which can almost always be produced in larger quantity by devoting more labor to the more intensive exploitation of land and mineral deposits that are already used in production, or by devoting labor to the exploitation of land and mineral deposits that are known but not presently exploited.[25])

For all practical purposes there is no limit to our need and desire for goods or, therefore, for the performance of the labor required to produce them. In having, for example, a need and desire to be able to spend incomes five or ten times the incomes we presently spend, we have an implicit need and desire for the performance of five or ten times the labor we presently perform, for that is what would be required in the present state of technology and the productivity of labor to supply us with such increases in the supply of goods. Moreover, almost all of us would welcome the full-time personal services of at least several other people. Thus, on both grounds labor is scarce, for the maximum amount of labor available to satisfy the needs and desires of the average member of the economic system can never exceed the labor of just one person. Indeed, in actual practice, it falls far short of that amount, because of the existence of large numbers of people, such as infants, small children, the elderly, and the sick, who are unable to work.

The consequence of the scarcity of labor is that *wage rates in a free market can fall no lower than corresponds to the point of full employment*. At that point the scarcity of labor is felt, and any further fall in wage rates would be against the self-interests of employers, because then a labor *shortage* would exist. Thus, if somehow wage rates did fall below the point corresponding to full employment, it would be to the self-interest of employers to bid them back up again. Essentially the same diagram [26]

These facts can be shown in the same supply and demand diagram I used to show the irrelevance to wage determination of workers being willing to work for subsistence. Thus, Figure 3 shows that if wage rates were below their market equilibrium of W_1, which takes place at the point of full employment, denoted by E—if, for example, they were at the lower level of W_2—a labor shortage would exist. The quantity of labor demanded at the wage rate of W_2 is B. But the quantity of labor available—whose employment constitutes full employment—is the smaller amount A. Thus, at the lower wage, the quantity of labor demanded exceeds the supply available by the horizontal distance AB.

The shortage exists because the lower wage of W_2 enables employers to afford labor who would not have been able to afford it at the wage of W_1, or it enables employers who would have been able to afford some labor at the wage of W_1 to now afford a larger quantity of labor. To whatever extent such employers employ labor that they otherwise could not have employed, that much less labor remains to

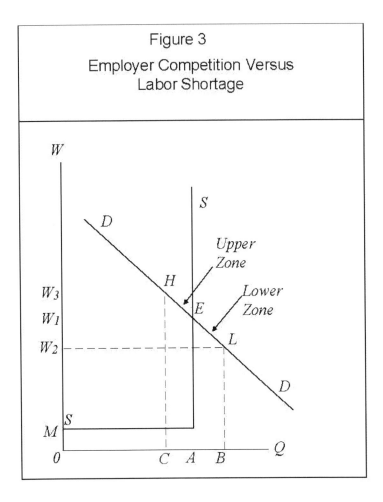

be employed by other employers, who are willing and able to pay the higher wage of W_1.

At the artificially low wage of W_2 the quantity AB of labor is employed by employers who otherwise could not have afforded to employ that labor. The effect of this is to leave an equivalently reduced quantity of labor available for those employers who could have afforded the market wage of W_1. The labor available to those employers is reduced by AC, which is precisely equal to AB. This is the inescapable result of the existence of a given quantity of labor and some of it being taken off the market by some employers at the expense of other employers. What the one set gains, the other must lose. Thus, because the wage is W_2 rather than W_1, the employers who could have afforded the market wage of W_1 and obtained the full quantity of labor A are now able to employ only the smaller quantity of labor C, because labor has been taken off the market by employers who depend on the artificially low wage of W_2.

The employers who could have afforded the market wage of W_1 are in identically the same position as the bidder at the art auction who is about to see the painting he wants go to another bidder not able or willing to pay as much. The way to think of the situation is that there are two groups of bidders for quantity AB of labor: those willing and able to pay the market wage of W_1, or an even higher wage—one as high as W_3—and those willing and able to pay only a wage that is below W_1—a wage that must be as low as W_2. In Figure 3, the position of these two groups is indicated by two zones on the demand line (or demand "curve"): an upper zone HE and a lower zone EL. The wage of W_1 is required for the employers in the upper zone to be able to outbid the employers in the lower zone.

The question is: Is it to the rational self-interest of the employers willing and able to pay a wage of W_1, or higher, to lose the labor they want to other employers not able or willing to pay a wage as high as W_1? The obvious answer is no. And the consequence is that if, somehow, the wage were to fall below W_1, the self-interest of employers who are willing and able to pay W_1 or more, and who stood to lose some of their workers if they did not do so, would lead them to bid wage rates back up to W_1. The rational self-interest of employers, like the rational self-interest of any other buyers, does not lead them to pay the lowest wage (price) they can imagine or desire, but the lowest wage that is *simultaneously too high for other potential employers of the same labor who are not able or willing to pay as much and who would otherwise be enabled to employ that labor in their place.*

The principle that it is against the self-interest of employers to allow wage rates to fall to the point of creating a labor shortage is illustrated by the conditions which prevail when the government imposes such a shortage by virtue of a policy of price and wage controls. In such conditions, employers actually conspire with the wage earners to evade the controls and to raise wage rates. They do so by such means as awarding artificial promotions, which allow them to pay higher wages within the framework of the wage controls.

The payment of higher wages in the face of a labor shortage is to the self-interest of employers because it is the necessary means of gaining and keeping the labor they want to employ. In overbidding the competition of other potential employers for labor, it attracts workers to come to work for them and it removes any incentive for their present workers to leave their employ. This is because it eliminates the artificial demand for labor by the employers who depend on a below-market wage in order to be able to afford labor. It is, as I say, identically the same in principle as the bidder who wants the painting at an auction raising his bid to prevent the loss of the painting to another bidder not able or willing to pay as much. The higher bid is to his self-interest because it knocks out the competition. In the conditions of a labor shortage, which necessarily materializes if wage rates go below the point corresponding to full employment, the payment of higher wages provides exactly the same benefit to employers.

I. 12. Marxism/Socialism as an Underlying Cause of Unemployment and Why the Fall in Wage Rates Required to Eliminate It Need Not Reduce Real Wages

I have referred several times to "full employment" and its importance in making the fundamental scarcity of labor felt and thus setting a competitive floor under wage rates. Full employment would be the norm in a capitalist economy. What prevents it is government intervention, primarily in the form of minimum-wage and prounion legislation. Such legislation again and again imposes increases in wage rates in the mistaken, Marxist/Socialist belief that the increases have no effect except to transfer funds from profits to wages—from capitalists to wage earners. When unemployment appears, whether as the result of this policy of government intervention or as the result of monetary contraction brought on by the government's policy of sanctioning and actually fostering prior credit expansion, the same Marxist/Socialist belief prevents the reductions in wage rates that would reestablish full employment.

Here it is necessary to point out that the fall in wage rates needed to establish full employment should not be feared as possibly serving to bring about the establishment of subsistence wages through the back door, so to speak. By this, I mean that so long as unemployment exists, there is room for wage rates to fall without the creation of a labor shortage. And in a free market, wage rates would in fact fall in such circumstances, until they reached the point of full employment. This is because in such circumstances, the self-interest of the employers, and also of the unemployed workers, would operate to drive them down. It should not be thought, however, that the fall in wage rates in these circumstances means that the conditions of supply and demand are capable of driving wages to minimum subsistence and thus creating the same human misery that Marxism attributes to the alleged arbitrary power of businessmen and capitalists over wages.[27]

The truth is that a drop in wage rates to the full employment point need not imply a drop in the average worker's standard of living. That is, it need not imply any reduction in the goods and services he can actually buy—any reduction in his so-called real wages. This is because the elimination of unemployment that the fall in wage rates brings about means both more production and a fall in costs of production, both of which mean lower prices. Indeed, if output per worker remained the same after the elimination of unemployment, the increase in the supply of products would be in the same proportion as the increase in employment. In the face of unchanged amounts of spending for consumers' goods and labor respectively, the fall in prices would be in the same proportion as the fall in wage rates.

Indeed, in this case, it is likely that real wages would actually rise with the elimination of unemployment, even in the short run. This is because not only can prices fall as much as wages, but also the burden of supporting the unemployed is eliminated. To the extent that, as a result, taxes are no longer deducted from workers' wages, or no longer negatively impact wages indirectly, the reduction in taxes means that disposable, take-home pay drops less than gross wages and less than prices.[28] When these facts are kept in mind, it is clear that insofar as market conditions require a fall in wage rates, the fall may well operate to raise the standard of living of the workers who are already employed, not reduce it.[29] An additional benefit to the workers who are already employed would be the elimination of the fear they must experience at the prospect of possibly losing their jobs and then finding no alternative jobs available to them. Full employment would ensure the existence of many alternative jobs being available.

*****

It is vital to understand that even in the midst of more or less substantial unemployment, imposed by government intervention, the tendency of capitalism is to go on increasing the supply of products produced while improving their quality and broadening their range, with the result that the real wages of all those who are employed go on increasing.[30]

*****

Keynes is famous for his claim that full employment is impossible under capitalism, irrespective of wage rates. His argument was that full employment means a higher level of production and real income. Out of the higher level of real income, there will be a higher level of saving, which in turn requires an equivalently higher level of net investment, to prevent the additional saving from being hoarded. But, says Keynes, as net investment increases, the rate of profit on capital decreases, and at the point of full employment so much net investment would be required to offset saving, that the rate of profit would be too low for investment to be worthwhile. Thus capitalism allegedly cannot have full employment because having it would mean an impossibly low rate of profit.[31]

As will be shown in Part III of this essay, contrary to Keynes, net investment and profit are not inversely related but positively related. Indeed, profit and net investment are almost the same thing in terms of their definitions. Profit is sales minus costs. Net investment is productive expenditure minus those very same costs. Productive expenditure, it will be shown, is the expenditure of business firms for capital goods and labor. The expenditure for capital goods is simultaneously a major portion of business sales revenues. The wage earners' spending out of their wages is also a major portion of business sales revenues. Thus an excess of productive expenditure over costs implies a virtually equivalent excess of sales revenues over costs, i.e., a virtually equivalent amount of profit.[32] As a result, it is only a short step to the conclusion that increases in net investment represent equal increases in the amount of profit in the economic system, thereby driving the rate of profit in the direction of 100 percent. The conclusion that follows is that whatever holds back profitability in the conditions of a depression and mass unemployment, it is not too much net investment but, if anything, not enough net investment. Thus, if, as Keynes claimed, the additional employment that results from a fall in wage rates would be accompanied by additional net investment, that would imply a restoration of business profitability, not its reduction from the already low or negative level of a depression. It would mean that a fall in wage rates was the solution both for overcoming mass unemployment and for restoring general business profitability.

I. 13. How Capitalism Progressively Raises Real Wages

Having established that at the point of full employment, wage rates cannot be reduced without creating a labor shortage, in which case the competitive bidding of employers would raise them right back up again, we can now turn to a step by step explanation of how capitalism raises the general standard of living and real wages in particular.

Capitalistic circulation begins when some workers in the conditions of simple circulation save a portion of their sales revenues and use them to employ helpers and to buy previously produced products for use in further production. In so doing they introduce a much higher degree of division of labor than could ever be possible under simple circulation. They increase the extent of the division of labor both horizontally and vertically. The addition of the labor of employees to that of sole proprietors or partnerships of proprietors makes possible a greater division of labor within the production of any given good. The presence of more hands makes possible the assignment of a smaller number of tasks as the specialized work of any given individual. With only one individual present, he must perform all of the tasks required in the production of what he produces and sells. With two individuals present, each need perform only half the necessary tasks. With twenty individuals present each need perform only one-twentieth of the necessary tasks. It depends on the volume of production and sales, of course, whether or not any given number of specific tasks is sufficient to constitute the full time work of any given individual.

At the same time, the purchase of previously produced products for use in further production extends the division of labor vertically. Part of the work required to produce a product is now performed by one's suppliers, and the work of one's own enterprise may now constitute part of the work required in producing the products of one's customers. The workers who make possible the horizontal and vertical expansion of the division of labor come to be known as businessmen and capitalists. They are responsible for the increase in production—the progressive increase in production—that is possible only in a division of labor economy.[33]

MARXISM/SOCIALISM, A SOCIOPATHIC PHILOSOPHY

At each step of the way, in order to gain employees, the businessmen and capitalists must offer them more in wages than the profits that they could earn on their own. Otherwise, those workers would refuse to become employees. And, as I have just shown, they must offer them more than any other potential employer is willing to offer them. It is this competition for labor by employers that the Marxists/Socialists call exploitation and slavery.

*****

The more economically capitalistic the economic system is, that is, the higher is M relative to M', the higher are wages relative to sales revenues and profits and the higher is the demand (expenditure) for capital goods relative to the demand for consumers' goods. These results follow from the fact that the rise in M is initiated by a fall in the consumption expenditure of the sellers of products, who now become capitalists by virtue of saving and then spending for capital goods and labor in order to earn future sales revenues greater than these expenditures. These newly self-created capitalists pay wages and buy capital goods instead of consuming. Consumption in the economic system as a whole, of course, falls by much less, because, to a major extent, new and additional consumption expenditure by wage earners takes the place of the reduced consumption expenditure on the part of capitalists; the savings of the capitalists finance the rise in wages and thus, indirectly, the rise in consumption on the part of wage earners.

The higher is the demand for capital goods relative to the demand for consumers' goods, the higher is the production of capital goods relative to the production of consumers' goods. A sufficiently high relative demand for and production of capital goods ensures that the production of new capital goods exceeds the using up of existing capital goods, with the result that the supply of capital goods increases. The increase in the supply of capital goods relative to the supply of labor makes possible a rise in the productivity of labor and thus an increase in production—an increase in the production both of consumers' goods and of further capital goods.

The higher is the economic degree of capitalism and thus the relative production of capital goods, the more likely is the economic system to be in a position to enjoy continuing economic progress and a rising productivity of labor and real wages on the strength of additional supplies of capital goods making possible the further increase in the supply of capital goods, along with further increases in the supply of consumers' goods. (This process requires continuing scientific and technological progress, which businessmen and capitalists are always on the lookout for and which they are often eager to finance. Such progress is necessary to counteract what would otherwise be a tendency toward diminishing returns to the employment of larger supplies of capital goods relative to labor.)

A major reason that a higher economic degree of capitalism contributes to a more rapid rate of economic progress is that the higher is the relative production of capital goods, the greater are the resources available in any given period of time for the production of products whose completion lies further in the future. For example, if 50 percent of the labor and capital goods of any given year are devoted to producing the consumers' goods of the following year, while the remaining 50 percent of the labor and capital goods of that year are devoted to producing the capital goods of the following year, then it follows that 25 percent of the labor and capital goods of that year will be devoted to the production of consumers' goods for the year after next—i.e., half to the capital goods of the following year, half of which are devoted to the production of the consumers' goods of the year after that. In the same way, only 12.5 percent of the labor and capital goods of any given year will be available to contribute to the production of consumers' goods not to be available for three years, and so on.

In contrast, if the relative production of capital goods were 60 percent instead of 50 percent, then the proportion of the labor and capital goods available in that year to contribute to the production of consumers' goods not to be available for three years would be .6 x .6 x .4 or 14.4 percent, instead of 12.5 percent. For consumers' goods not to be completed for four years, the proportions of resources available in the present year to contribute to their production would be 6.25 percent for the 50/50 relative production of capital goods and consumers' goods and 8.64 percent for the 60/40 relative production of capital goods and consumers' goods. For consumers' goods not to be available for ten years, the respective proportions would differ by more than fourfold.

Such differences greatly impact the kinds of technologies an economic system is capable of adopting. The greater the resources available in any given year for the achievement of temporally more remote results, the greater is the range of technologies it can adopt. An economy in a state of simple circulation—zero economic degree of capitalism—would have great difficulty producing anything beyond a rock and a stick. In contrast, the highly capitalistic (both economically and politically) economies of nineteenth century Britain and the United States had the resources available to construct bridges and tunnels requiring years of work, build steel mills to produce thousands of miles of steel rails, produce thousands of pieces of rolling stock and locomotives, roundhouses and train stations—all on the foundation of their vastly higher economic degree of capitalism and correspondingly greater concentration on the relative production of capital goods. This advantage of greater resources available for the achievement of temporally more remote results had a major positive impact on all branches of the economic system.

The continually rising productivity of labor that a sufficiently high economic degree of capitalism brings about when it is coupled with scientific and technological progress, causes a continuing increase in the buying power of wages, i.e., a continuing rise in "real wages." As already explained, the rise in the economic degree of capitalism raises wages relative to sales revenues and profits, but the rise in the buying power of wages caused by the rise in the productivity of labor is far more important in explaining the rise in the standard of living of wage earners under capitalism. This is because the productivity of labor, and with it, real wages, are capable of being doubled and redoubled from generation to generation. This has essentially been the story of the United States, Great Britain, and Western Europe since the start of the Industrial Revolution. More recently, it has been the story of Japan, South Korea, Taiwan, and, since its adoption of essential features of capitalism, much of mainland China too. In comparison, once wages have come to exceed profits several times over, no further increase in wages relative to profits could accomplish more than a relatively modest further increase in real wages.

The way that the rise in the productivity of labor raises real wages is by virtue of making the supply of goods more and more abundant relative to the supply of labor and thereby progressively reducing prices relative to wages. In reality, the increase in the supply of goods is almost always accompanied by an increase in the quantity of money and thus in the volume of spending in the economic system. This is what serves to increase money wages. But the increase in the quantity of money and volume of spending also serves more or less equally to raise prices. What allows real wages—the buying power of wages—to rise in the face of an increasing quantity of money and volume of spending is that the increase in the supply of goods relative to the supply of labor serves to make the rise in prices less than the rise in wages. If the increase in money and spending is modest, as it is under a gold standard, the effect is likely to be merely to reduce the extent of the fall in prices, while money wages rise.

I. 14. How Capitalism Shortens the Working Day, Abolishes Child Labor, and Improves Working Conditions

The rise in the productivity of labor, and consequent rise in real wages that capitalism achieves is what shortens the hours of work and abolishes child labor. As businessmen and capitalists succeed in raising the productivity of labor and real wages higher and higher, more and more wage earners come to be in a position in which they can afford to accept the lower wages that accompany a shorter work day and work week. In 1780, at the beginning of the Industrial Revolution many workers worked 80 hours a week to earn bare minimum subsistence. By the time that businessmen and capitalists had succeeded in doubling or tripling the real wages of an 80-hour workweek, most workers were put in a position in which they could afford to accept the lower pay that accompanies a substantially shorter work week. They could now afford to work just a 60-hour week, say, and earn three-fourths of what they might have earned, because, even so, they were still very substantially better off than they had been. Three-fourths of twice subsistence is one and a half times subsistence. Three fourths of three times subsistence is two and a quarter times subsistence. Indeed, the workers came to be in a position in which they could even afford to work for wages reduced in greater proportion than the hours they worked, thereby making a shorter workweek a source of lower costs per unit of labor than the old, longer workweek, and making it positively more profitable for employers to adopt it. (The other side of the coin of a discount on the wages of shorter hours is a premium on the wages of longer hours. Thus, in effect, the free market itself creates a need to pay "overtime," if one will, on hours in excess of the hours that most workers have come to prefer.)

As the rise in the productivity of labor and real wages continued, the work week continued to fall—from 60 hours a week to 48 hours, to 40 hours, and to less than forty hours. If full-bodied capitalism existed and were allowed to continue, the work week would fall still further.

Capitalism abolishes child labor by virtue of the fact that as the real wages of parents rise, families become less and less dependent on any financial contribution that their children might make. They can thus afford to keep their children home longer and longer. Nowadays, in the United States at least, there are children who do not begin working until the age of twenty-five.

Child labor has existed since caveman days. Historically, everyone's labor was required in the struggle for bare existence. It's true that in the early days of capitalism, there were children working as young as the age of four. This was not the fault of capitalism. It was the heritage of human history. Throughout the nineteenth and twentieth centuries, capitalism proceeded to raise the age at which child labor began: from four to seven, to ten, to twelve, to fourteen… and now, in more than a few cases, twenty-five.

Improvements in working conditions come about in essentially the same way as the shortening of hours. Namely, the rise in real wages puts more and more workers in a position in which they can afford to accept wages that are lower by enough to offset the costs of employers paying for the improvements in cases in which the improvements do not pay for themselves. Improvements in working conditions often do pay for themselves by increasing productivity. In cases of this kind, employers will install them just as they would install anything else that paid for itself through its contribution to production, such as, typically, machinery. Contrary to what Marxists/Socialists appear to believe, employers have no prejudice against things that improve working conditions and make life easier for wage earners, provided they pay for themselves. Thus, if a particular kind of machinery that employers were planning to install made it possible for workers to experience less fatigue, say, that would not make employers want to install it any the less.

But let us imagine a package of amenities that does not pay for itself through increasing output per worker; say, a combination of summer air conditioning, convenient modern lavatories, and the presence of certain basic safety features. Let us assume that providing these amenities costs, say, $1,000 per worker per year. Given the level of real wages in a country like the United States, whichever employers offered these amenities would be able to attract workers at annual wages lower than the $1,000 per year it costs to provide them. By the same token, in comparison with jobs that had these amenities, jobs that did not have them would be considered extremely undesirable, and could attract labor only at a substantial premium in wage rates. Thus it would clearly be to employers' self-interest to provide them, as a means of reducing their overall labor costs. From the perspective of employers, it would be less expensive to pay the $1,000 annual cost per worker and avoid having to pay a premium in wage rates of $2,000 or more per worker per year that would be needed to attract labor in the absence of these amenities.

The situation is very different in countries in which real wages are extremely low, as in India and Southeast Asia. There the cost of having such comforts as air-conditioning and modern lavatories, and even minimally safe working conditions, may be as much as these workers earn altogether, or, at the very least, equal to a substantial fraction of what they earn altogether. Workers in such a position simply cannot afford to work for wages lower by enough to cover the employers' costs of providing such improvements. They need every last penny of their employers' expenditures on account of labor that they can put in their pockets and spend—on things they consider more urgent than comfort and safety at work, such as minimal food and clothing for themselves and their families. But as capitalism raises their real wages and eliminates their hunger and puts clothing on their backs and shoes on their feet, and continues to raise their real wages further and further, the point is reached at which they can afford to accept wages that are lower than the wages they could otherwise put in their pockets and spend. They can more and more accept wages that are lower by enough to cover the part of the cost of air-conditioning, modern lavatories, on-the-job safety, and the like, that does not pay for itself through its contribution to production.

I. 15. Implication of Harmful Effects of Government Interference with Hours and Conditions of Work

It follows from this discussion that government interference in the economic system that compels shorter hours, a higher minimum age for working, or improvements in working conditions, has the effect of forcing on very poor people what for them are luxuries that they are as yet unable to afford, and thereby makes their lives even harder than they already are.

Inasmuch as, under capitalism, the hours of work, child labor, and working conditions are all ultimately the result of the free choices of the wage earners, based on their consideration of what they can and can't afford, the government's compelling their choices is comparable to its sending its agents out to Robinson Crusoe's island and ordering him to work fewer hours than he has decided he needs to work, or compelling him to divert his labor from the production of such necessities as food and clothing to providing for improvement in his working conditions, or compelling Swiss Family Robinson to reduce the labor that in its judgment it is necessary for its children to perform. In all such cases, it is a matter of the ignorant and arrogant ordering other people to act against their self-interests for no reason other than that people who are utterly ignorant of how other's self-interests are actually served are arrogant enough to pretend that nevertheless they can serve the self-interests of those others better at the point of a gun than those others can serve their own self-interests on the basis of their own thought and actual knowledge of their circumstances.

I. 16. Fallacy of the Marxists'/Socialists' Belief that to Benefit from the Means of Production, People Need to Own Them

The ignorance of the Marxists/Socialists concerning capitalism is present in their belief that the privately owned means of production under capitalism serve exclusively their owners and no one else. And in the further belief that the great mass of people, who are non-owners of the means

MARXISM/SOCIALISM, A SOCIOPATHIC PHILOSOPHY

of production, or at least not very substantial owners, can benefit from them only by first becoming owners, i.e., by seizing the means of production, establishing socialism, and thereby becoming collective owners of the means of production.

The fact is that under capitalism the privately owned means of production *serve the market* and thus that everyone benefits from them who buys their products. The physical benefit that derives from the existence of automobile factories, the steel mills that supply them, and the iron mines that feed the steel mills—the actual physical benefit of all these privately owned means of production goes to the buyers of automobiles, who need not own a single dollar of the capital that is invested in any of them. The same, of course, is true throughout the economic system. The physical benefit of a capitalist economy's privately owned means of production all goes, directly or indirectly, to the general buying public, which, for the overwhelmingly greater part, consists of wage earners.

The portion of a capitalist economy's final product—its automobiles, food, clothing, television sets, and all other consumers' goods—that goes to wage earners, as opposed to businessmen and capitalists, is the greater, the more economically capitalistic is the economic system, i.e., the higher is M/M'.[34] That first M, and the wage payments included in it, is the higher relative to M', the smaller is the portion of spending that is constituted by consumption expenditures on the part of businessmen and capitalists, who own and sell the products and thus collect the second M, the M'. For the businessmen and capitalists use the overwhelming bulk of the sales revenues that come in at the end of one sequence of M-C-M` to constitute the first M of the next sequence, i.e., to buy the labor and capital goods used in the next sequence, and not to consume.

Thus, under capitalism, the privately owned means of production are the source of the supply of consumers' goods that the great wage earning mass of the population buys and of the demand for the labor that it sells. Also, the more economically capitalistic the economic system, the higher are wages and the consumption of wage earners relative to profits and the consumption of businessmen and capitalists, and, at the same time, the greater and more rapidly increasing is the supply of consumers' goods for everyone to buy.

Moreover, under capitalism in order to gain back in sales revenues the outlays for labor and capital goods that they have made, let alone earn a profit, the businessmen and capitalists must please their customers, who spend their funds where they choose and believe they are best served. This forces the businessmen and capitalists to compete with one another in introducing new and improved products and in finding ways to reduce the costs, and thus the prices, of producing existing products, success in either of which will induce buyers to buy from them and hopefully allow them to be profitable enough to grow richer and expand.[35]

In contrast, under socialism, production is in the hands of men who have no incentive to make profits or avoid losses. For they cannot personally grow richer or poorer by doing so, since under socialism the means of production are the property of the state, not of individuals. Not having an incentive to make profits and avoid losses, they have no incentive to compete with one another. And, indeed, not being the owners of means of production, they have no authority to change the ways in which they are used in the first place, which means that they cannot act on their own, individual initiative. Thus production under socialism is characterized by lack of incentives, lack of competition, and lack of individual initiative. Production under socialism is so ossified that it might as well be a system of production in the hands of zombies. But since conditions in the world are forever changing and thus fresh thought and action are continually needed, which socialism cannot supply, socialism must ultimately collapse into a state of hunger and starvation.

I. 17. How Capitalism Is Run for the Benefit of the Masses while Socialism Is Run for the Benefit of the Ruling Elite at the Cost of Starvation Wages

I have shown that under capitalism wages are determined by the competition of employers for labor. Businessmen and capitalists are compelled by the market either to pay more for the labor they need than their next nearest competitors or go without that labor. Under socialism there is no competition of employers for labor. Under socialism, there is only one employer, the State, which holds a universal monopoly on employment and which prohibits any possible competition with it by making anyone else's ownership of means of production illegal. Under these conditions, the conditions of socialism, the only necessary wage is a wage that keeps the citizens alive and able to work, i.e., minimum subsistence.

Even if it had the ability, a socialist state has no reason to pay wages to the general population that are above minimum subsistence. It may pay more in special circumstances, where the work is of special value to the state by helping to maintain its power or prestige—for example, the work of scientists developing new weapons of mass destruction, the work of secret police agents, and the work of star athletes and performers that serves to bring prestige to the regime. The status of the ordinary citizens of a socialist society is implied in the moral/political premise that the individual is the means to the ends of society. Since "society" is not a real entity and cannot be communicated with in any actual way, what this proposition means is that the individual is the means to the ends of society *as divined by the rulers of society*. The meaning of *this* proposition is that *under socialism the individual is the means to the ends of the rulers*.

The rulers care nothing for the well-being of the common man. They have a million things on their minds that they consider to be more important. The well-being of the common man, in their estimation, is never of greater importance than the value of a good "photo-op." In sharpest contrast, however, *businessmen and capitalists* do pay the most careful and prolonged attention to improving the well-being of the common man. They literally stay up late at night thinking of ways to produce better and less expensive products for use in every aspect of life. They do this work not out of any altruistic love of mankind, which is what the socialists claim about themselves (and which morons think is morally superior and economically more efficient). They do it, rather, as the means of making a personal fortune, in the knowledge that it is for such accomplishments that masses of ordinary men and women will pay them.

Under capitalism everyone is an end in himself. At the same time the pursuit of self-interest by the capitalists provides a supply of means of production that results in a supply of goods and a demand for labor that enriches everyone. The payment of wages, which are the higher relative to profits, interest, and dividends, the more economically capitalistic is the economic system, enables the wage earners, through their "buying and abstention from buying," to use the words of the great von Mises, to exercise decisive economic power over the capitalists and to make them conduct the economic system preponderantly for the benefit of the wage earners—a result implied by the far greater volume of consumer spending coming from wage earners than from capitalists.

Thus, under capitalism, the capitalists work for the benefit of the masses. Under socialism, the masses toil for the benefit of the ruling elite.

I. 18. Fallacy of the Marxists'/Socialists' Belief that Capitalism Lacks Planning and Is an "Anarchy of Production"

The ignorance of the Marxists/Socialists concerning capitalism is equally present in their belief that capitalism lacks economic planning, that it is "an anarchy of production," and that the establishment of socialism is necessary to bring rational, planned order out of the alleged chaos of capitalism.

The truth is that capitalism is full of economic planning. Everyone who goes to any kind of store with a shopping list is engaged in economic planning: he's planning to buy the items on his list. Everyone is engaged in economic planning. Consumers are planning to buy homes and automobiles, and a million and one other things, and also to save for the future, often planning to save in order to buy the things they are planning to buy. Wage earners are planning to find a new job or stay in their present one, to learn new skills, or rest content with the one's they have. Everyone is planning to move or remain where he is. Businessmen are planning to open new stores and build new factories, or to close existing ones. They are planning to hire additional workers or let some of their present workers go. They are planning to increase their inventories or reduce their inventories. They are planning to change their methods of production or continue with the ones they presently use. They are planning to add new products to their offerings or eliminate some of the products they presently offer.

Indeed, economic planning is present in all of the thinking that people do that relates to improving their performance as buyers or sellers. It is all of the thought that serves to enable people to earn more money and spend less money for anything they buy. It includes planning all of the details involved in providing anything they sell, including all of the aspects of its production. People must plan to follow each of the steps that it is necessary for them to follow in order to provide whatever it is that they sell. In short, under capitalism, everyone is engaged in economic planning, in all the ways described in this and in the preceding paragraph, and more.

Yet when a Marxist/Socialist looks at the economic activities of other people, he has absolutely no understanding of what they are doing or why. To him, it is just chaos—an "anarchy of production." To him, it is as though other people did not have minds. They are all engaged in an allegedly mad scramble to get the most and give the least. He, the Marxist/Socialist certainly has no idea of what people are doing. They are all just crazy in his view. His level of knowledge of economics, of how the profit motive, competition, and the price system coordinate, harmonize, and integrate the plans of hundreds of millions, indeed, billions of separate individuals into a cohesive, highly workable, and prosperity-creating whole is literally at the level of a moron.

The integration of the plans of separate individuals into a harmonious whole needs illustration. Thus, for example, imagine that halfway around the world, people have carried out their plan to build a new major highway between a seaport and highly fertile agricultural land. Farmers in that region can now make and carry out plans for a large-scale increase in their production of various crops. The suppliers of these farmers will have to revise their plans in order to accommodate the additional demand for various goods and services that these farmers and their employees will be making. And so too will the suppliers of these suppliers, and their suppliers,

Soon after our farmers' plans come to fruition, the prices of the kinds of crops they produce will fall in world markets, because of the increase in their supply and the consequent need to attract additional buyers through the offer of lower prices. In the face of these lower agricultural prices, farmers elsewhere in the world must rethink their activities, because the fall in their selling prices will have reduced their profits. They must now either plan how to reduce their costs of production, in order to restore their profits, or plan what else they might produce, which might entail their giving up agriculture altogether. To the extent that they do decide to give up agriculture, their arrival in other lines of production, will operate to reduce prices and wages in the fields they enter. That will require planning on the part of those already in these fields, who must now contend with the lower prices and wages.

At the same time, the lower prices of agricultural products will operate to leave more money in people's pockets, that they will now have available to buy goods, or additional quantities of goods, that they previously could not afford. People will plan how best to spend their additional available funds. And depending on how and where they spend them, the sales revenues and profits of a wide variety of firms will now increase. The sellers here will have to plan how to meet the additional demand that now faces them. And so too will their suppliers, and their suppliers'

suppliers, as additional demand filters back through the process of production.

As a second example of the extent of economic planning under capitalism, consider such a thing as the periodic reductions and threatened reductions in the supply of oil that have taken place over the years, as the result of the actions of the OPEC cartel in an environment in which the American oil and other energy producing industries had to operate under strangling government regulations, including price controls. Under capitalism and its uncontrolled price system, a reduction in the supply of a commodity such as oil, serves to raise its price. The rise in the price of oil represents an increase in the cost of production of all oil products, which is then passed on in a rise in the prices of oil products, e.g., gasoline, heating oil, and jet fuel.

Indeed, not only will the price of oil products rise, but so too the prices of physically very disparate goods that depend on the use of oil or oil products in their production, such as most forms of travel, the generation of electricity, and the products of many factories that use oil or oil products for heating or power. In response to the rise in these prices, all of the individual buyers of the various products whose prices have risen must consider what their alternatives are to the use of those products and turn to them as substitutes when it is feasible to do so. The choices of the hundreds of millions, perhaps billions, of buyers of all the products directly or indirectly dependent on the use of oil as to where to cut back and by how much, determines which oil products, and, in the same way, which further products of those various oil products, are produced in reduced quantity and by how much, and in which particular geographic locations the supply reductions are carried out and to what extent. Thus, here we have a process of thinking and planning on the part of perhaps the majority of the world's population that determines the response to the reduction in the supply of oil.

What these examples illustrate is not only that capitalism has economic planning on the part of everyone, but also that every significant change in economic conditions results in the *replanning* of the economic system by everyone affected by the change. In contrast, socialism is supposed to be able to succeed on the basis of the planning of just one man, the Supreme Dictator, or at most a relative handful of men, the members of the "central planning board." They will run the economy on the basis of *one plan* that in Soviet Russia was supposed to be good for *five years*. (In Nazi Germany, the government's plan was supposed to be good for four years.)

As I've written elsewhere concerning alleged economic planning under socialism, "By its nature, this attempt to make the brains of so few meet the needs of so many has no more prospect of success than would an attempt to make the legs of so few the vehicle for carrying the weight of so many. To have rational economic planning, the independent thinking and planning of all are required, operating in an environment of private ownership of the means of production and the price system, i.e., capitalism."[36] And, as I have just shown, what is also required is the continuous *rethinking and replanning* of the economic system by everyone who participates in it. Capitalism is as rich in economic planning compared to socialism as it is in material goods.[37] The reason for this is that the alleged economic planning of socialism is in fact not economic planning at all, but the *forcible suppression of economic planning*—the forcible suppression of the economic planning of everyone in the economic system outside the membership of the central planning board, which holds a government imposed monopoly on economic planning. Only its members are allowed to think and plan. Forcibly turning off the thinking and planning of billions is Marxism's/Socialism's formula for success.

*****

I have shown that under socialism, the only necessary wage for the great mass of workers is a wage that keeps them alive and able to work, i.e., minimum subsistence. But because of its ossification and lack of actual economic planning, in other words, its "anarchy of production," to apply an expression of Marx's appropriately for once, socialism, to paraphrase Marx, cannot even maintain its slaves in their slavery: the workers of socialism sink deeper and deeper into poverty—to borrow two more of Marx's false claims about capitalism and apply them truthfully, in application to socialism. Thus, it is socialism, not capitalism, that is the system of subsistence wages—until its ossification, general economic chaos, and anarchy of production drive wages below subsistence and millions of people die of starvation.

I. 19. Enslavement under Socialism

In sharpest contrast to capitalism, a socialist state effectively enslaves the workers and makes them mere means to the ends of the ruling elite. It does so, first of all, by means of the initiation of physical force against all other, potential employers, whose activities are simply prohibited. Their potential competition for labor is made a criminal offense on the grounds that if it were allowed to exist, the workers would be "exploited." Thus, in a perfect display of Marxist/Socialist logic, the competition that would put an end to the exploitation of labor by the socialist state is prohibited on the grounds that it would introduce the exploitation of labor. Of course, the socialist state's prohibition of employment by anyone but itself serves to forcibly hold the workers in service to it, as much as if they were chained to their jobs.

On top of this, in response to the universal shortages that accompany its economic chaos, and necessitate that it decide which products it is more important to produce than others, the socialist state again and again decides where specifically workers will work, whether they want to or not.[38] In the Soviet Union, millions of them were sent to work in openly slave-labor concentration camps in Siberia. Workers in the Soviet Union were prohibited from leaving their jobs without permission from their state employers. All university and technical school graduates were compulsorily assigned to a job for a period of two to three years following graduation.[39]

Indeed, forced labor is implied in the very nature of the socialist state's attempting to plan production. The socialist state's deciding what and where which goods are to be produced, in what quantities and by what methods, implies plans about the disposition of the labor that is to produce them. If, for example, so many million tons of iron ore and other minerals are to be extracted from various locations in Siberia, a commensurate number of workers with the necessary skills must be present in those locations to extract the minerals. Does anyone believe that the socialist state will induce them to go there by offering them higher wages, and perhaps signing bonuses as well? And to make the higher wages and bonuses meaningful, introduce into its economic plans the construction of the housing, shops, movie theaters, and the like on which the higher wages and bonuses could be spent?

Nothing compels a socialist state to behave in this way. Unlike capitalists, if, after it makes its best offer (or any offer), it still cannot find the workers it needs to fill the jobs called for by its plans, it does not have to accept the decision of workers not to take these jobs as final. Being the state, it has at its disposal an inducement that capitalists do not have at their disposal. Namely, *physical force*. It can go out and arrest the workers it needs and ship them to where it wants them to work. After all, as the Marxists/Socialists see things, these workers will then just be working where "Society" needs them. And who are they to place their personal, selfish concerns about comfort and the like above the needs of Society? Society will be gaining according to its needs, while the workers are contributing according to their abilities. Can anyone imagine a more just and moral arrangement? Or, in the view of normal people, who are not sociopaths, a more *un*just and *im*moral arrangement?

I. 20. The Necessity of Terror under Socialism[40]

A fundamental fact that explains the totalitarianism and all-round reign of terror found under socialism, in such countries as the Soviet Union and Communist China, is the incredible dilemma in which a socialist state places itself in relation to the masses of its citizens. On the one hand, it assumes full responsibility for the individual's economic well-being. This is the main source of its popular appeal. On the other hand, in all of the ways one can imagine, a socialist state makes *an unbelievable botch of the job*. While it promises planning and order, it delivers chaos and anarchy, making the individual's life a nightmare.

Every day of his life, the citizen of a socialist state must spend time in endless waiting lines. For him, the problems Americans experienced in the gasoline shortages of the 1970s are normal; only he does not experience them in relation to gasoline—for he does not own a car and has no hope of ever owning one—but in relation to simple items of clothing, to vegetables, even to bread. Even worse he is frequently forced to work at a job that is not of his choice and which he therefore must certainly hate. (For, as mentioned just a few paragraphs ago, under shortages the government comes to decide the allocation of labor just as it does the allocation of the material factors of production.) And he lives in a condition of unbelievable overcrowding, with hardly ever a chance for privacy. (In the face of housing shortages, strangers are assigned to homes; families are compelled to share apartments. And a system of internal passports and visas is adopted to limit the severity of housing shortages in the more desirable areas of the country.) To put it mildly, a person forced to live in such conditions must seethe with resentment and hostility.

Now against whom would it be more logical for the citizens of a socialist state to direct their resentment and hostility than against that very socialist state itself? The same socialist state which has proclaimed its responsibility for their life, has promised them a life of bliss, and which *in fact* is responsible for giving them a life of hell. Indeed, the leaders of a socialist state live in a further dilemma, in that they daily encourage the people to believe that socialism is a perfect system whose bad results can only be the work of evil men. If that were true, who in reason could those evil men be but *the rulers themselves,* who have not only made life a hell, but have perverted an allegedly perfect system to do it?

It follows that the rulers of a socialist state must live in terror of the people. By the logic of their actions and their teachings, the boiling, seething resentment of the people should well up and swallow them in an orgy of bloody vengeance. The rulers sense this, even if they do not admit it openly; and thus their major concern is always to keep the lid on the citizenry.

Consequently, it is true but very inadequate merely to say such things as that socialism lacks freedom of the press and freedom of speech. Of course, it lacks these freedoms. If the government owns all the newspapers and publishing houses, if it decides for what purposes newsprint and paper are to be made available, then obviously nothing can be printed which the government does not want printed. If it owns all the meeting halls, no public speech or lecture can be delivered which the government does not want delivered. But socialism goes far beyond the mere lack of freedom of press and speech.

A socialist government totally *annihilates* these freedoms. It turns the press and every public forum into a vehicle of hysterical propaganda in its own behalf, and it engages in the relentless persecution of everyone who dares to deviate by so much as an inch from its official party line.

The reason for these facts is the socialist rulers' terror of the people. To protect themselves, they must order the propaganda ministry and the secret police to work 'round the clock. The one, to constantly divert the people's attention from the responsibility of socialism, and of the rulers of socialism, for the people's misery. The other, to spirit away and silence anyone who might even remotely suggest the responsibility of socialism or its rulers—to spirit away anyone who begins to show signs of thinking for himself. It is because of the rulers' terror, and their desperate need to find scapegoats for the failures of socialism, that the press of a socialist country is always full of stories about foreign plots and sabotage, and about corruption and mismanagement on the part of subordinate officials, and why, periodically, it is necessary to unmask large-scale domestic plots and to sacrifice major officials and entire factions in giant purges.

It is because of their terror, and their desperate need to crush every breath even of potential opposition, that the rulers of socialism do not dare to allow even purely cultural activities that are not under the control of the state. For if people so much as assemble for an art show or poetry reading that is not controlled by the state, the rulers must fear the dissemination of dangerous ideas. Any unauthorized ideas are dangerous ideas, because they can lead people to begin thinking for themselves and thus to begin thinking about the nature of socialism and its rulers. The rulers must fear the spontaneous assembly of a handful of people in a room, and use the secret police and its apparatus of spies, informers, and terror either to stop such meetings or to make sure that their content is entirely innocuous from the point of view of the state.

Socialism cannot be ruled for very long except by terror. As soon as the terror is relaxed, resentment and hostility logically begin to well up against the rulers. The stage is thus set for a revolution or civil war. In fact, in the absence of terror, or, more correctly, a sufficient degree of terror, socialism would be characterized by an endless series of revolutions and civil wars, as each new group of rulers proved as incapable of making socialism function successfully as its predecessors before it. The inescapable inference to be drawn is that the terror actually experienced in the socialist countries was not simply the work of evil men, such as Stalin, but springs from the nature of the socialist system. Stalin could come to the fore because his unusual willingness and cunning in the use of terror were the specific characteristics most required by a ruler of socialism in order to remain in power. He rose to the top by a process of socialist natural selection: the selection of the worst.

In sum, socialism is totalitarian by its very nature.

I. 21. From Enslavement to Mass Murder under Socialism[41]

I have described socialism as entailing enslavement. Enslavement under socialism easily turns into mass murder. To understand how this happens, we must contrast enslavement under socialism with enslavement under different conditions.

Slavery existed in ancient Greece and Rome and in the Southern United States before the Civil War, and was, of course, a moral abomination. Nevertheless, abominable as slavery was, there was an important factor in these cases which restrained the slave owners and the overseers in their treatment of the slaves. That was the fact that *the slaves were private property.* A private slave owner was restrained in his treatment of his slaves by his own material self-interest. If he injured or killed his slave, he destroyed his own property. Of course, out of ignorance or irrationality, this sometimes happened; but it was the exception rather than the rule. Private slave owners were motivated to treat their slaves with at least the same consideration they gave to their livestock, and to see to it that their overseers acted with the same consideration.

But under socialism, the slaves are "public property"—the property of the state. Those who have charge of the slaves, therefore, have no personal economic interest in their lives or well-being. Since they are not owners of the slaves, they will not derive any personal material benefit if the slaves are alive to work in the future, nor suffer any personal material loss if the slaves are not alive to work in the future. In such conditions, slave labor results in mass murder. The officials in charge of the slaves are given orders to complete certain projects as of a certain time. Quite possibly, they are threatened with being reduced to the status of slaves themselves, if they fail. In these circumstances, the slaves are treated as valueless natural resources. Brutal punishments are inflicted on them for trifling reasons, and they are worked to the point of exhaustion and death. The slaves of socialism are slaves, but they are no one's property and therefore no one's loss.

In this way, slave labor under socialism results in mass murder. In just this way, tens of millions of people have been murdered.

Of course, the economics of slavery under socialism is not a sufficient explanation of mass murder. Those who participate in the system must be utterly depraved. But observe how socialism creates the conditions in which depravity flourishes—the conditions in which depravity can express itself, is freed of the restraints of better motives, and is positively nurtured and encouraged. For it is socialism that delivers men into slavery. It is socialism that removes the restraint of self-interest from those in charge of the use of any form of property. And it is socialism that creates an environment of the hatred and punishment of all by all—"as a way of getting back at the system for the hardship and frustration they themselves have suffered."[42] In such conditions, the most depraved and vicious element of the population finds a place for its depravity and viciousness and steps forward to run the labor camps and the whole socialist society.

In addition to the transformation of forced labor into mass murder under socialism, there is the further fact that socialism cannot rationally plan and so exists in a state of chronic chaos. Nor do its citizens have the incentive to produce. In this state, the production of essential commodities can easily be radically insufficient, with the result that, as I have shown, even if it wanted to, socialism cannot maintain its slaves in their slavery and the masses of workers sink deeper and deeper into poverty, which at some point means that they die. The former Soviet Union would have suffered tens of millions more deaths caused by the economic chaos of socialism, had not the outside, capitalist world, principally the United States, repeatedly bailed it out with massive food shipments and guaranteed loans, and again and again served as the source of all kinds of emergency supplies. And millions can die also as the result of political calculations by the ruling elite in which the lives of the millions count for nothing, as was the case in Soviet Russia and Communist China in instances of planned famines there.

Thus, socialism begins and ends with murder—murder to establish it, in stealing the means of production from their capitalist owners; murder to maintain it economically and politically, through slave labor without any incentive to keep the slaves alive, and the sacrifice of scapegoats for its failures; and, finally, murder as the product of its very existence and consequent economic chaos and impoverishment, and its utter lack of concern for the value of human life, which it regards as merely an egg needing to be broken, in order to make an omelet—the omelet that is socialism.

PART II. MARX'S LABOR THEORY OF VALUE LUNACY

Having presented and refuted the gist of Marx's exploitation theory in the first part of this essay, it is now time for me to turn to some of the major details of his lengthy exposition of the theory, an exposition that includes not only the eight-hundred pages of volume one of *Das Kapital*, but the additional pages of volumes two, three, and four, as well as the text of *The Communist Manifesto*, and other writings. This will confirm Marx's profound ignorance of economics, his blindness to facts, his intellectual dishonesty, and a pattern of thinking that suggests a series of grudges against capitalists and capitalism manufactured for no other purpose than that of arousing hatred against them and seemingly justifying robbing and murdering them.

II. 1. What Marx Ignores to Get to His Labor Theory of Value and the Exploitation Theory

In the course of expounding the exploitation theory, Marx presents his version of the labor theory of value, a version that is very different from the one presented by the classical economists, most notably Smith, Ricardo, and John Stuart Mill. Marx simply ignores the role of supply and demand in the determination of prices, not only in the case of rare consumers' goods, such as paintings by old masters, but also, and much more importantly, in the determination of wage rates, real estate prices, and the prices of many raw materials, all of which prices between them play a major role in determining the costs of production of products. He ignores the role both of the rate of profit and the period of time that must elapse between outlays for means of production and receipts from the sale of products, during which time the rate of profit compounds. He ignores the role of the differences in wage rates between workers of different degrees of skill, and the role of differences in wage rates between workers of the same degree of skill working in different countries.[43] On the basis of this massive and willful blindness to economic reality, he then arrives at the conclusion that:

> Commodities, therefore, in which equal quantities of labour are embodied, or which can be produced in the same time, have the same value. The value of one commodity is to the value of any other, as the labour-time necessary for the production of the one is to that necessary for the production of the other. "As values, all commodities are only definite masses of congealed labour-time."[44]

II. 2. The Implication that the Product of an Hour's Labor by a Brain Surgeon Has the Same Value as that of an Hour's Labor by a Gardener, and the Dishonesty of Marx's Attempt to Defend this Absurd Claim

One leading implication of the above passage is that the value of the product of an hour of labor by a brain surgeon is the same as the value of the product of an hour of labor by a gardener.

Marx has what he thinks is a way to defend such absurdities. He writes:

> Skilled labour counts only as simple labour intensified, or rather, as multiplied simple labour, a given quantity of skilled labour being considered equal to a greater quantity of simple labour. . . . For simplicity's sake we shall henceforth account every kind of labour to be unskilled, simple labour; by this we do no more than save ourselves the trouble of making the reduction.[45]

So, according to Marx, the brain surgeon, whose hourly wage may be a thousand times that of the gardener and who can afford to live in a mansion, own a yacht, and dine on champagne and caviar, is, in reality, the equivalent of a thousand gardeners living at the level of minimum subsistence.

II. 3. Further Implications: Only Fresh Labor Adds Value and the Value of Labor Itself Is Determined by the Quantity of Labor Required to Produce It

Having laid down his principle that "The value of one commodity is to the value of any other, as the labour-time necessary for the production of the one is to that necessary for the production of the other," Marx arrives at the further conclusion that the only way that products can be more valuable than the previously produced means of production used up to produce them is through the addition of fresh labor. For example, the only thing, according to Marx, that explains why a loaf of bread is more valuable than the flour and the other items used up in producing it, including a portion of the depreciation on the ovens and bakery, is that the bread is the product of more labor than they contain. All the labor that they contain, and contribute to the bread passes over into the bread, but the bread is the product of more labor than that. It contains, in addition, the labor applied in the bakery to or with the aid of those means of production. The resulting additional value, the value added, allegedly all by the fresh labor performed in the bakery, is then divided between wages and profits.

What determines this division, according to Marx, is a further application of his insane version of the labor theory of value, an application that places the free workers of capitalism in the identical position as slaves, as discussed early in the first part of this essay:

> The value of labour-power [i.e., what the worker must be paid—GR] is determined, as in the case of every other commodity, by the labour-time necessary for the production,

and consequently also the reproduction, of this special article. So far as it has value, it represents no more than a definite quantity of the average labour of society incorporated in it. Labour-power exists only as a capacity, or power of the living individual. Its production consequently presupposes his existence. Given the individual, the production of labour-power consists in his reproduction of himself or his maintenance. For his maintenance he requires a given quantity of the means of subsistence. Therefore the labour-time requisite for the production of labour-power reduces itself to that necessary for the production of those means of subsistence; in other words, the value of labour-power is the value of the means of subsistence necessary for the maintenance of the labourer.[46]

I repeat the last portion of Marx's last sentence: "the value of labour-power is the value of the means of subsistence necessary for the maintenance of the labourer." The question must be asked, does a brain surgeon require a thousand times more means of subsistence than a gardener? Or is he, besides being a brain surgeon, also a thousand gardeners? Or is there simply no connection between his wages and the value of the goods whose consumption is essential for him to have the ability to perform brain surgery?, in which case his wages can exceed the value of those goods a thousand times over. The obvious answer is that there is simply no connection between his wages and the value of the goods necessary for him to do his work. Nor is there any necessary, direct connection between the wages of any worker and his means of subsistence.[47]

Because of his evasion of the existence of skilled labor, through counting it as a multiple of "simple labour," Marx is able to ignore the fact that what he has written about wages being determined by subsistence has absolutely no application, even in the framework within which he writes, to skilled workers of any kind—that their wages are not at all determined by "subsistence" or the quantity of labor needed to produce "subsistence," and that therefore there is no reason why any worker's wages has to have any kind of direct, permanent, or automatic connection with "subsistence."

Nevertheless, according to Marx, the capitalist employer pays the worker only the subsistence-value of his labor and then gains to the extent that the worker works more hours than is equivalent to the hours required to produce his subsistence. Those hours are "surplus-labour time," which is the alleged source of "surplus-value" and profit. Observe how Marx's account has exactly recreated the conditions of slavery, in which the master (now the capitalist employer) gains from the slave's (now the worker's) ability to produce more than is required to keep himself alive.

II. 4. Marx's Claim that Subsistence Wages Are Permanent under Capitalism

According to Marx, there is no escape from workers' receiving only subsistence wages under capitalism. This is because, according to Marx, to the extent that the capitalists succeed in reducing the quantity of labor required to produce the wage earner's necessities, the capitalists then proceed to cut wages to the same extent, so that the wage earner is left in exactly the same position as before, and, at the same time, the capitalists are able to increase their profits to the extent of the alleged reduction in wages. Marx writes:

> [I]f, in consequence of increased productiveness, the value of the necessaries of life fall, and the value of a day's labour be thereby reduced from five shillings to three, the surplus-value increases from one shilling to three. Ten hours were necessary for the reproduction of the value of the labour-power; now only six are required. Four hours have been set free, and can be annexed to the domain of surplus-labour. Hence there is immanent in capital an inclination and

constant tendency, to heighten the productiveness of labour, in order to cheapen commodities, and by such cheapening to cheapen the labourer himself.[48]

Restating Marx's example in simpler terms, what he has just said is that the working day is twelve hours long. Initially, ten hours are required to produce the wage earner's necessities. If for every hour of labor embodied in products, including the wage earner's necessities, there were one dollar of product value, the wage earner's twelve hours of labor would add twelve dollars to the value of the materials and depreciation on plant and equipment entering into the products he produced. Because he himself had to be paid ten dollars to be able to buy his necessities, which require ten hours of labor in their production and thus sell for ten dollars, the capitalist's profit or "surplus-value" was two dollars, corresponding to the two hours of "surplus-labor" the worker performed—i.e., the labor he performs over and above the amount of labor required to produce his necessities. Now, however, the capitalists succeed in being able to have the wage earner's necessities produced with only six hours of labor instead of ten. The effect of this is to reduce the price of those necessities from ten dollars to six dollars.

Now the actual further effect of such a development would be a rise in the buying power of the worker's ten dollars of wages by two-thirds. At a price of six dollars for his necessities instead of ten dollars, the worker's ten dollars of wages would now be sufficient to buy not only his necessities, but also a further amount of goods equal in value to two-thirds of his necessities. In other words, his real wages—the buying power of his wages—would rise to one and two-thirds of their initial height (ten dollars in wages divided by six dollars for the goods he had been buying).

However, Marx claims that the capitalists somehow have the power arbitrarily to cut wages, just because, and to the extent that, the prices of the wage earner's necessities fall. Marx's claim contradicts the fact that once any particular type of labor in any given location is fully employed, any further fall in its wage rates would result in a labor shortage, as I showed in an earlier section of this essay.[49] At that point, capitalists able and willing to pay more could not obtain the labor they wanted because it was employed by other capitalists not willing or able to pay as much, with the result that wages would be bid back up or not fall in the first place because of the realization that it would deprive employers of needed labor.

Marx's dishonesty in ignoring skilled labor and its wages allows him to avoid the question of why the capitalists cannot reduce those wages along with the alleged reduction in the wages of "simple labour." What stops the capitalists from cutting the wages of skilled workers as the prices of necessities and the other items that they buy fall? Why haven't the capitalists already reduced the wages of skilled workers to the level of minimum subsistence in the first place? The actual answer, of course, which Marx never permitted himself even to suspect, is that such wage reductions would result in labor shortages, with the results described in the preceding paragraph. And if, because of these facts, it is not possible for the capitalists to reduce the wages of skilled labor once the point of its full employment has been reached, then because of the very same facts, it is not possible for the capitalists to reduce the wages of unskilled, simple labor, once its point of full employment has been reached.

II. 5. Marx's Unintended Concession Concerning the Economic Role of Capitalists and His Delusional Interpretation of It

It is necessary to repeat the last line in Marx's claim that subsistence wages are permanent under capitalism because the capitalists use the fall in the prices of the workers' necessities that results from increases in productiveness to then cut their wages.[50] Recall that Marx has said, "Hence there is immanent in capital an inclination and constant tendency, to heighten the productiveness of labour, in order to cheapen commodities, and by such cheapening to cheapen the labourer himself."

Here Marx concedes that capitalism operates to raise the productivity of labor. We have seen that it does so by virtue of the profit-incentive the capitalists have to cut the costs of production and to introduce new and improved products, and by virtue of their freedom of individual initiative and their mutual competition.[51] Reductions in the wage earners' cost of living are the cumulative result of such improvements brought about by numerous individual capitalists. Here Marx implicitly acknowledges all this, but, according to him, it's not enough for the individual capitalist just to increase his own profits and thus personal wealth through successful innovation and competition, accompanied by a fall in the selling price of his product.

No. The individual capitalist has to be part of *a conspiracy of capitalists*, each one working for the purpose of making possible an increase in the profits of the capitalist *class* at the expense of the wages of the working class. Thus, the capitalists responsible for improvements in the methods of production that bring about a fall in the price of clothing or flour, say, have allegedly developed these improvements not for the purpose of themselves earning high profits and thereby growing rich, but rather for the purpose of enabling the capitalist class to cut wages. They have made clothing and flour cheap, in order "to cheapen the labourer," says Marx."

To put it mildly, this is delusional, conspiratorial thinking on the part of Marx.

II. 6. Marx's Claim of Progressive Impoverishment: Capitalists' Greed and a Falling Rate of Profit

Not only are the workers condemned to subsistence wages forever, according to Marx, but under capitalism, things go from bad to worse. They are allegedly driven there by a combination of the capitalists' insatiable greed for "surplus-value" (profit) and by the fact, according to Marx, that the only capital that adds value and thus "surplus-value" is the portion used to pay wages. This follows from Marx's primary proposition that quantity of labor is the only value creating substance. According to Marx, the capital invested in materials, machines, factory buildings, and the like, yields no profit, because it allegedly creates no additional value. Only additional labor, says Marx, can create additional value and thus create profit, to the extent that the value it creates exceeds what is necessary for the wage earners' subsistence. Because the capital invested in things other than the payment of wages allegedly creates no value, Marx calls it "constant capital," as opposed to the wage-paying part of capital, which he terms "variable capital."[52,53]

Marx claims that, apart from more variable capital being needed to pay subsistence wages to a larger population, capital accumulation takes place in the form of a growth in constant capital. The effect of this is to require that the same amount of surplus-value be spread over a larger total volume of capital invested, which implies that the rate of profit, i.e., the amount of surplus-value divided by the amount of capital invested, must progressively fall as more constant capital is accumulated. According to Marx, this alleged fall in the rate of profit is added to the inherent greed of the capitalists and drives them to increase the degree of their alleged exploitation of labor in order to offset the fall in the rate of profit by providing additional surplus value.[54]

II. 7. The Absurdity of Marx's Proposition that only the Wage-Paying Part of Capital Yields Profit

Marx's proposition that only the part of capital that pays wages—his so-called variable capital—yields profit, is, of course, absurd. If true, it would mean that investments in such labor-intensive lines of business as restaurants and barbershops would be far more profitable than investment in capital-intensive lines of business, such as power plants, steel mills, and automobile factories. The truth is, as Smith and Ricardo established long before Marx, all branches of production tend to earn the same rate of profit. This is because insofar as some industries are more profitable than others, capital tends to move from the less profitable industries into the more profitable ones, which serves to raise up the rate of profit in the former and bring it down in the latter. The rate of profit rises in industries from which capital is withdrawn if for no other reason then because the reduced output of these industries can be sold at higher, and thus more profitable, prices, while the increased output of the industries in which additional capital is invested must be sold at lower, and thus less profitable, prices.[55]

Marx's proposition, along with the underlying claim that only labor creates value, which is the core of his version of the labor theory of value, also shows ignorance of such

MARXISM/SOCIALISM, A SOCIOPATHIC PHILOSOPHY

well-known facts of reality as that $100 of capital invested in raw whiskey stored in casks to age, and without the employment of any additional labor whatever, will be worth $148 in eight years and more than $700 in forty years, if the rate of profit is 5 percent per year. And with a 10 percent annual rate of profit, the value of the eight-year old whiskey would be more than $200, while that of the forty-year old whiskey would be more than $4,500. Likewise, capital invested in power plants, steel mills, and automobile factories, earns profit on its entirety, not just on the relatively small portion of capital invested, in the payment of wages. It appears as though Marx never bothered to read David Ricardo, who elaborated on cases of this kind at considerable length. And, in introducing Section IV of his chapter "On Value," Ricardo wrote, "The principle that the quantity of labour bestowed on the production of commodities regulates their relative value considerably modified by the employment of machinery and other fixed and durable capital"—modified, in other words, by the fact that Marx's so-called "constant capital" is not constant at all, but yields profit and thereby brings it about that the performance of the same quantity of labor can result in products of very unequal value.[56]

Marx claimed to have read Ricardo, and devoted more than two hundred pages to discussing his views. But his answer here is essentially unintelligible: the introduction of a distinction between commodity "values," which are allegedly still determined strictly and only by the relative quantities of labor required to produce the commodities, and "prices of production," which take into account the influence of the rate of profit and the period of time for which it compounds, but which nevertheless allegedly do not qualify as actual commodity values, according to Marx.[57]

II. 8. Marx's Claim that the Capitalists' Greed and a Falling Rate of Profit Result in an Increase in the Rate of Exploitation and in the Length of the Working Day

Both because of their greed and in order to hold back the alleged fall in the rate of profit resulting from the growth of "constant capital," the capitalists, says Marx, increase the rate of exploitation, i.e., the amount of surplus-value relative to the wage payments needed to provide subsistence to the workers. That way, says Marx, there will be more surplus-value to spread over the growing total of capital invested. In particular, Marx claims, they lengthen the working day, which serves to increase the difference between the value added by fresh labor and the worker's subsistence wage, which wage is allegedly sufficient to enable him to work longer hours and thereby create additional surplus-value for the capitalist.

In effect, according to Marx, the capitalists see the workers lolling about after work in pubs or amusing themselves on playing fields, expending energy that the food provided by the capitalists has made possible. Instead of allowing that energy to be wasted in such idleness, the capitalists will allegedly capture it in the factories, in the production of commodities, where it can add to the magnitude of surplus-value. They allegedly accomplish this by reducing hourly wages, thereby compelling the workers to work longer hours to earn subsistence. The result is a corresponding rise in the amount and rate of "surplus-value," and an accompanying offset to the fall in the rate of profit. If, for example, the working day can be extended to eighteen hours from twelve hours, while the worker still requires necessities produced in only six hours, then the rate of surplus-value is increased from 100 percent to 200 percent. For s/v^{58} = *surplus labor/necessary labor* = $(18 - 6)/6 = 200$ percent. Thus, the rate of profit can allegedly be doubled, or at least maintained in conditions in which it would otherwise have been cut in half.[59]

Concerning the length of the working day, Marx writes:

> "What is a working day? What is the length of time during which capital may consume the labour-power whose daily value it buys? How far may the working day be extended beyond the working time necessary for the reproduction of labour-power itself?" It has been seen that to these questions capital replies: the working day contains the full 24 hours with the deduction of the few hours of repose without which labour-power absolutely refuses its services again.... It is not the normal maintenance of the labour-power which is to determine the limits of the working day; it is the greatest possible daily expenditure of labour-power, no matter how diseased, compulsory, and painful it may be, which is to determine the limits of the labourers' period of repose.... Capital cares nothing for the length of life of labour-power. All that concerns it is simply and solely the maximum of labour-power, that can be rendered fluent in a given working day. It attains this end by shortening the extent of the labourer's life, as a greedy farmer snatches increased produce from the soil by robbing it of its fertility.[60]

Of course, in arguing that the capitalists increase the length of the working day, Marx contradicts the fact that the rising real wages made possible by the capitalists bring about a shortening of the working day, as previously shown.[61] Marx is unaware of such facts because he is lost in a fantasy world of a conspiracy of capitalists to reduce wages every time they succeed in increasing the productivity of labor and reducing the price of necessities, as though this, not the profits they made from the increases in productivity, were the purpose of the increases. Had Marx looked at the facts, he would have seen that the increases in the productivity of labor that the capitalists brought about served in fact progressively to raise real wages and thereby to shorten the working day.

II. 9. Marx's Claim Concerning the Capitalists' Appropriation of the Labor of Women and Children Through the Use of Machinery

The greed for "surplus-value," claims Marx, leads the capitalists to appropriate the labor of women and children in exactly the same way as they appropriate the additional hours of labor of the adult males. Namely, they reduce wage rates and thereby make it necessary for a wage earner's entire family to perform labor in order to earn enough for the family to obtain subsistence. In this way, once again, the expenditure of energy made possible by the food the capitalists enable the workers to buy is allegedly captured in the production of commodities and thus in the generation of "surplus-value."[62]

Marx describes this alleged phenomenon in the following passages, in which he blames machinery for making such exploitation possible:

> In so far as machinery dispenses with muscular power, it becomes a means of employing labourers of slight muscular strength, and those whose bodily development is incomplete, but whose limbs are all the more supple. The labour of women and children was, therefore, the first thing sought for by capitalists who used machinery. That mighty substitute for labour and labourers was forthwith changed into a means for increasing the number of wage-labourers by enrolling, under the direct sway of capital, every member of the workman's family, without distinction of age or sex....
>
> [Before the coming of machinery, t]he value of labour-power was determined, not only by the labour-time necessary to maintain the individual adult labourer, but also by that necessary to maintain his family. Machinery, by throwing every member of that family on to the labour market, spreads the value of the man's labour-power over his whole family. It thus depreciates his labour-power. To purchase the labour-power of a family of four workers may, perhaps, cost more than it formerly did to purchase the

labour-power of the head of the family, but, in return, four days' labour takes the place of one, and their price falls in proportion to the excess of the surplus-labour of four over the surplus-labour of one. In order that the family may live, four people must now, not only labour, but expend surplus-labour for the capitalist. Thus, we see, that machinery, while augmenting the human material that forms the principal object of capital's exploiting power, at the same time raises the degree of exploitation.[63]

What Marx is saying here is that initially the capitalist paid an adult male worker six dollars a day for twelve hours of work.[64] Those six dollars were sufficient for the worker to feed himself, his wife, and two replacement children. They corresponded to the six hours of labor required to produce the necessities consumed by the worker and his family. At the same time, the worker's twelve-hour day added twelve dollars to the materials used up and depreciation incurred in the process of producing the worker's product, leaving a further six dollars over as "surplus-value" or profit, corresponding to the worker's six hours of "surplus-labor"—six hours of labor over and above the labor necessary to produce subsistence for himself and his family.

Now, because machinery makes it possible for the worker's wife and children to find employment in a factory somewhere, the capitalist can reduce the male worker's wage from six dollars a day to one-fourth of six dollars a day, i.e., to a dollar and fifty cents a day. The plunge in the adult male worker's wage will then force his wife and two replacement children into the labor market, where they will also each earn a dollar and fifty cents a day. In this way, the family's daily earnings will be restored to six dollars a day, but instead of only twelve hours of labor being performed by one adult male worker, and only six dollars of surplus-value being generated, there will now be four workers working a combined total of forty-eight hours and all for the same original subsistence wage of just six dollars. The alleged result is that the four workers together add forty-eight dollars of value to the capitalist's materials and depreciation, but still collectively receive just six dollars of wages. Thus, instead of just six hours of surplus-labor-time being performed and six dollars of surplus-value being generated, there are now forty-two hours of surplus-labor-time being performed and forty-two dollars of surplus-value being generated. The "rate of exploitation," i.e., the ratio of "surplus-labor-time" to "necessary labor time" or, equivalently, the ratio of "surplus-value" (profit) to wages thus rises from one-hundred percent to seven hundred percent—i.e., from $6 of profit divided by $6 of wages, to $42 of profit divided by $6 of wages.

In his treatment of the labor of women and children, Marx contradicts the fact that capitalism abolishes child labor by virtue of increasing the real wages of parents and thus progressively reducing their need for any financial contribution from their children, as was shown in a previous section.[65] He also ignores the fact that women being able to work in factories served to give women a major measure of financial independence, which they had not previously had. And he contradicts the fact that their now being able to work substantially increased the real incomes of their families. For their earnings did not take the place of a portion of their husbands' previous earnings but were added to the earnings of their husbands, thereby increasing the income of their families.

II. 10. An Additional Absurd Claim by Marx: Cheapening the Worker's Diet

Yet another alleged method of raising the rate of "surplus-value," according to Marx, is a cheapening of the worker's diet.⁶⁶ If the workers could be forced to substitute potatoes or rice for more expensive food, the so-called necessary labor time would be reduced and "surplus-labor-time" correspondingly increased.

In reading Marx, it is difficult to avoid reaching the conclusion that, in his view, if the capitalists could operate openly, without restraint of any kind, there would be a section in the financial pages of the newspapers that does not presently appear—namely, a listing of the prices of such wage earners' necessities as rice, potatoes, and loincloths, and the rentals of cardboard shanties and mud huts. The capitalists, supposedly, would read this section every day and then adjust wages to reflect reductions in these prices.⁶⁷

This page intentionally left blank.

Part III. THE ACTUAL DETERMINANTS OF PROFIT AND THE RATE OF PROFIT

Profit has nothing to do with the quantity of labor required to produce products or with the quantity of labor required to produce the wage earners' necessities. Nor, therefore, does it have anything to do with Marx's so-called "surplus-value."

Ironically, however, Marx's formulations of "simple circulation" and "capitalistic circulation," which go back to Adam Smith and which are implicit in the principles of business accounting, can play a role in understanding the subjects of profit and the rate of profit. When they do, they also destroy virtually every other aspect of his system of thought.

In order to be as clear as possible, let me say that in the pages that follow what I will be attempting to explain is how it is possible for all the individual business firms in the economic system taken together regularly and consistently to show an excess of sales revenues over costs, and what determines the amount of this aggregate excess. Let me say also that when I speak of the rate of profit in the economic system, what I mean is the system-wide amount of profit, as expressed in the aggregate of business firms' income statements, divided by the system-wide amount of capital invested, as expressed in the aggregate of the balance sheets of business firms, specifically in their inventory/work in progress accounts and in their net plant and equipment accounts. Thus, to find the rate of profit, we add up the profits of all the business firms that have profits and subtract the sum of the losses of all the business firms that have losses, and then divide the result by the sum of all business firms' inventory/work in progress accounts and their net plant and equipment accounts. Strictly speaking, the asset "cash" in the possession of business firms should also be included in the calculation of their capital. Its inclusion, of course, enlarges the denominator in the equation for the average rate of profit and thus serves somewhat to reduce the economy-wide average rate of profit.[68]

Because interest is an income very similar to profit and is a target of Marxism/Socialism along with profit, I exclude interest payments to individuals from the costs deducted from sales revenues and thus take profits gross of these interest payments. In this way, interest can be seen to be determined in fundamentally the same way as profit.

III. 1. The Prime Cause of Profit: Expenditure to Buy Commodities

What gives rise to the phenomenon of profit is *expenditure to buy commodities*. This is the source of sales revenues. If the sellers then use their sales revenues simply to consume, i.e., if they buy not for the purpose of subsequently selling, but for any purpose other than subsequently selling, their expenditures generate further sales revenues, and the process can be endlessly repeated in Marx's simple circulation sequence C-M-C, i.e., workers producing commodities, C, selling them for money, M, and then using the proceeds to buy other commodities, C. Here, as I have shown, the entire sales proceeds are profit, because while there are sales revenues there are no costs of production to deduct from them.[69]

This finding, of course, is in full and direct opposition to Marx, Adam Smith, and almost everyone else, even including Marx's greatest and best known critic, the Austrian-school economist Eugen von Böhm-Bawerk. They all believe that in the circumstances of "simple circulation" and Adam Smith's "original state of things," all income is wages and that profit emerges only later, with the coming of capitalists, and that when it emerges it does so as a deduction from what was originally, naturally, and rightfully all wages. (Böhm-Bawerk argues that profits are a justified deduction from wages, inasmuch as the capitalist enables the wage earner to receive payment immediately upon completion of his work, rather than have to wait for the sale of his ultimate product, which might be years in the future.[70])

III. 2. The Origin of Costs to be Deducted from Sales Revenues

Given the knowledge that profit, not wages, is the original and primary form of income— the income that is earned in "simple circulation" or Adam Smith's "original state of things," simply on the basis of the existence of sales revenues—the key question concerning profit now becomes not the origin of profit, but the origin of *costs*.

Costs originate when simple circulation begins to be transformed into capitalistic circulation. That transformation starts and intensifies as sellers use part, and then more and more, of their sales revenues for the purpose of earning sales revenues. In Marx's terms, this is the beginning and intensification of capitalistic circulation, M-C-M`—the outlay of money, M, for the purpose of producing commodities, C, which are then to be sold for a further and larger sum of money, M`.

Once this sequence begins, a number of new, highly relevant phenomena appear, in addition to or alongside those already explained in connection with capitalistic circulation.[71] The first is what I call "productive expenditure," i.e., expenditure for the purpose of making subsequent sales. It is identical with the first M in Marx's sequence of capitalistic circulation. Productive expenditure is distinguished from consumption expenditure by the fact that productive expenditures are made *for* the purpose of making subsequent sales, while consumption expenditures are made *not* for the purpose of making subsequent sales.

III. 3. Productive Expenditure, Sales Revenues, and Costs

Productive expenditure has two components: an expenditure for goods and an expenditure for labor, which latter is wage payments. The goods purchased by productive expenditure are *capital goods* or, equivalently, producers' goods, a term not used as frequently. The labor purchased by productive expenditure could be termed "capital labor" or equivalently, "producers' labor." The latter seems to be easier for people to accept than the former. I am accustomed to using the terms capital goods and producers' labor as the respective objects of the two components of productive expenditure.

Like productive expenditure, consumption expenditure also has two components: expenditure for consumers' goods and expenditure for consumers' labor. Consumers' labor is labor employed not for the purpose of making subsequent sales. The leading examples are personal servants and government employees.[72]

Productive expenditure has a twofold relationship to profits: It generates both sales revenues and the costs deducted from sales revenues.

The capital goods component of productive expenditure constitutes sales revenues automatically and instantaneously. For example, the purchase of steel sheet by an automobile company is a productive expenditure from its perspective and simultaneously a sales revenue from the perspective of the steel company that sells it the steel sheet. The producers' labor component of productive expenditure is not automatically and simultaneously a sales revenue. However, it is almost certain that it will very soon become sales revenues, as the wage earners spend their wages. Thus we can reasonably assume that all of productive expenditure directly or indirectly shows up as sales revenues.

For the sake of simplicity, I ignore such complications as the possibility that the wage earners might hoard a portion of their wages, or dis-hoard wages that were previously hoarded. For the same reason, I also ignore any saving on their part that would serve to increase productive expenditure.[73]

Productive expenditure not only comes back to the economic system as sales revenues but it also sooner or later shows up as costs in business income statements, which costs must be deducted from sales revenues. The costs will be in the form of "cost of goods sold" to the extent that the productive expenditures are for merchandise that will be sold or for materials and labor that are used to produce goods that will be sold. They show up in the form of "depreciation cost" insofar as the productive expenditures are for plant and equipment. And, finally, productive expenditures appear as costs in the form of what I call "expensed expenditures," that is, all the instances in which the productive expenditures are not added into the balance sheet accounts of "inventory/work in progress" or "plant and equipment" but go immediately into the income statement as costs. Expensed expenditures can be taken as synonymous with the category "selling, general, and administrative expenses." They include such things as executives' salaries, lighting and heating bills, and advertising expenses.

Productive expenditures are always tending to become costs in business income statements, and sooner or later they do become such costs, though sometimes not for decades. For example, money spent to construct a building with a depreciable life of forty years will not fully show up in costs until forty years have passed following the building's completion. In the interval, one-fortieth of the building's cost will show up in the firm's income statement year after year, for forty years.

III. 4. Productive Expenditure, Costs, and Net Investment

Productive expenditure for inventory/work in progress or for plant and equipment represents equivalent additions to the accounting value of these assets, while cost of goods sold and depreciation represent equivalent subtractions from the respective accounting values of these assets. As a result, any positive difference between productive expenditure and income-statement costs constitutes a net addition to the value of these assets. It represents, in other words, *net investment,* and thus an increase in accumulated capital as it appears on business balance sheets.

Thus, productive expenditure for merchandise, materials, and manufacturing labor constitutes an equivalent addition to the balance sheet asset inventory/work in progress. Cost of goods sold constitutes an equivalent subtraction from the accounting value of this asset. Consequently, an excess of such productive expenditure over cost of goods sold constitutes a net increase—net investment—in inventory/work in progress.

In the same way, productive expenditure for plant and equipment constitutes an addition to the accounting value of the balance sheet asset "gross plant and equipment." At the same time, depreciation constitutes an addition to the balance sheet item "accumulated depreciation reserve," which is subtracted from the gross plant and equipment account to arrive at the "net plant and equipment" account. Thus any excess of productive expenditure for plant and equipment over depreciation means an addition to a minuend that is greater than the addition to the subtrahend. The result is that the difference between the two numbers, in this case, the net plant account, is equivalently increased, which, in turn means, net investment in plant and equipment and thus capital accumulation as it appears on business balance sheets.

The remaining item of productive expenditure and of the costs subtracted from productive expenditure is "expensed expenditures." Since this item is equally present in both productive expenditure and in the costs subtracted from productive expenditure, it does not affect the amount of the difference between them, nor, therefore, the amount of net investment.

III. 5. The Tendency toward Productive Expenditure and Income-Statement Costs Becoming Equal

If the same amount of productive expenditure took place in the economic system year after year for capital goods and producers' labor, and if there were no tendency for the lapse of time between the making of the productive expenditures and their appearance as costs in business income statements continually to increase, then productive expenditure and costs would become equal at some point. For example, if every year there were the same amount of productive expenditure for assets with a one year life, a five year life, a ten year life, and a forty year life, then by the end of forty years the annual depreciation costs stemming from all these assets would equal the unchanged annual productive expenditure for such assets.

For example, if year after year, there were the same amount of productive expenditure for buildings with a depreciable life of forty years, then at the end of forty years there would be forty batches of such assets. Even though in any given year the depreciation cost on any one batch would be only one-fortieth of the cost of constructing it, the depreciation cost resulting from forty batches of such assets would equal the full cost of constructing such a batch. Meanwhile, the depreciation cost on account of assets with shorter lives would already have equalized with the full cost of new such assets, and that equality would have been repeated year after year since the time it was first achieved, and would now continue on into the future.

Similarly, again with the same amount of productive expenditure year after year, if the period of time that elapsed between the purchase of merchandise and its sale remained the same, and the period of time that elapsed between the purchase of materials and labor for the production of goods to be sold, and their sale, remained the same, ranging from the case of buying food for a restaurant which will show up in meals that are sold within days, to the production of aged whiskey not to be ready for sale until decades had passed—if this took place, then cost of goods sold in the economic system would come to equal productive expenditure on account of inventory and work in progress in the economic system. This is because a time would be reached at which point the productive expenditures of the present, however remote from becoming income-statement costs in the future, would be accompanied by income-statement costs reflecting productive expenditures made equally far back in the past.

Now given these two assumptions—repetition of the same amount of productive expenditure and maintenance of the same interval of time between the making of productive expenditures and their showing up as income-statement costs—we reach the conclusion that at some point, profit in the economic system would equal the difference between sales revenues and productive expenditure. For profit is sales revenues minus costs, and here costs, which are generated by productive expenditure, equal productive expenditure.

The equality of productive expenditure and income-statement costs does not actually require that year after year productive expenditure remain the same for each and every particular period of time that must elapse between its being made and its showing up as a cost in a business income statement. Thus, it does not require that productive expenditure remain the same for assets specifically with a one year life, a five year life, and so on. What it requires is merely that the economy-wide average lapse time stop increasing, so that in the face of any given overall amount of productive expenditure, there will be an overall amount of income-statement costs equal to it. This is consistent with many individual industries and many investments with different periods of lapse time showing an excess of productive expenditure over costs, i.e., net investment, and others showing an overall equivalent excess of costs over productive expenditure, i.e., negative net investment. The essential point that needs to be recognized is, as I put it just a moment ago, that in the face of economy-wide income-statement costs coming to equal economy-wide productive expenditure, "profit in the economic system would equal the difference between sales revenues and productive expenditure. For profit is sales revenues minus costs, and here costs, which are generated by productive expenditure, equal productive expenditure."

III. 6. Net Consumption: The Excess of Sales Revenues over Productive Expenditure

We can now go further. For observe that sales revenues and productive expenditure contain a common component, namely, expenditure for capital goods. Sales revenues equal the sum of expenditure for consumers' goods plus expenditure for capital goods. Productive expenditure, of course, is the sum of expenditure for capital goods plus expenditure for producers' labor. If we subtract from the sum of expenditure for consumers' goods plus expenditure for capital goods, the sum of expenditure for capital goods plus expenditure for producers' labor, expenditure for capital goods disappears and we are left with the difference between expenditure for consumers' goods and expenditure for producers' labor.

Thus, in the conditions assumed, in which the costs that appear in business income statements have grown to equality with productive expenditure, *profit equals the difference between the expenditure for consumers' goods and the expenditure for producers' labor.* [74] I have termed this difference *net consumption*.[75, 76]

The source of net consumption is sales revenues, just it was in the conditions of Marx's simple circulation, when the consumption of the sellers of products generated sales revenues that were one-hundred percent profit, because of the absence of productive expenditure and hence of costs to deduct from sales revenues. The consumption of the sellers of products, who are now businessmen and capitalists, is still derived from sales revenues, via draw payments in the case of partnerships and sole proprietorships and dividend payments in the case of corporations. None of these payments count as costs in business income statements. The expenditure of all of them, however, is a source of sales revenues to others and enables sales revenues to exceed productive expenditures in the economic system.

As I explained at the beginning of this part of my essay, because interest is an income very similar to profit and is a target of Marxism/Socialism along with profit, I exclude interest payments to individuals from the costs deducted from sales revenues and thus take profits pre-deduction of these interest payments. In this way, interest can be seen to be determined in fundamentally the same way as profit and profit can be seen as the source out of which interest is paid. However, while I exclude interest payments to individuals from costs, I include those interest payments as a source of consumption expenditure by their recipients and thus of the earning of sales revenues by others.

In this way, allowing for dividends, draw, and interest payments, there is, in the midst of capitalistic circulation, a continuing element of simple circulation, as it were. Businessmen and capitalists are in part producing commodities C, to be sold for money, M, and then using the money to buy other commodities, C. This continuing "simple circulation element," so to speak, is the main factor responsible for the existence of profit under capitalistic circulation. It is what makes M` greater than M—that is, it is what makes sales revenues in the economic system greater than productive expenditure and thus greater than income-statement costs equal to productive expenditure.

To put it slightly differently, the businessmen and capitalist sellers of products use their sales revenues to make two kinds of expenditures: productive expenditure, which is the relatively greater the more economically capitalistic the economic system is, and consumption expenditure. *These two types of expenditure together generate fresh sales revenues in the economic system that are equal to the combined total of these two types of expenditure. But only the productive expenditure portion generates costs to be deducted from those sales revenues.* In this way, businessmen and capitalists are responsible for the fact that sales revenues in the economic system regularly and consistently exceed productive expenditure and thus regularly and consistently exceed income statement costs equal to productive expenditure.

In still other words, profits under capitalistic circulation are the result of the fact that capitalistic circulation, or, better, the economic degree of capitalism—M/M′—*is less than one-hundred percent.* The amount by which M is less than M` is, in the long run, the amount by which productive expenditure and its resulting equivalent income-statement costs are less than sales revenues, which, of course, is the amount of net consumption and thus profit in the economic system.

To put it yet still another way, M represents the portion of their sales revenues that the sellers of products productively expend, while the amount by which M lags behind M` is the amount by which the recipients of M` consume their funds rather than productively expend them. M` is continually regenerated by the combination of the funds that its recipients consume and the funds that they productively expend. But only the portion that they productively expend shows up as costs.

The amount by which the economic degree of capitalism falls short of one-hundred percent is the continuing source of profit in the economic system and determines the rate of profit in the economic system. For example, in the conditions of Marx's simple circulation or, equivalently, Adam Smith's "original state of things," the rate of profit is infinite, for there is a positive amount of profit, equal to the totality of sales revenues, and zero accumulated capital, owing to the absence of productive expenditure and thus of sums of money being expended for plant and equipment or inventory and work in progress. With no money expended for these assets, their accounting asset value is zero. The rate of profit that is equal to any positive amount of profit, let alone to the totality of sales revenues, divided by zero is infinity.

By the same token, the higher is the economic degree of capitalism, the lower is the rate of profit, for the greater productive expenditure relative to sales revenues means not only ultimately higher costs to be deducted from sales revenues, thereby reducing the amount of profit in the economic system. It also means more spending for business assets and a more or less prolonged period in which such spending exceeds costs, during which time net investment and the accumulation of capital on the balance sheets of business occur. This increase in accumulated capital, combined with a decrease in the amount of profit in the economic system resulting from a higher economic degree of capitalism, constitutes a fall in the economy-wide average rate of profit.

III. 7. Net Investment and Its Disappearance

Until income-statement costs and productive expenditure equalize, net investment is a component in the economy-wide amount of profit. For profit equals sales minus costs, which in turn equals sales minus productive expenditure, which is net consumption, plus productive expenditure minus costs, which is net investment.

However, with a constant state of time preference in the economic system and a fixed quantity of money and volume of spending for capital goods and producers' labor, net investment would ultimately disappear. For productive expenditure would cease to grow and the lapse of time between the making of productive expenditures and their showing up as costs in business income statements would also cease to increase. Thus income-statement costs and productive expenditure would become equal.

The meaning of time preference: Time preference is the preference for consumption in the present over consumption in the future and for consumption in the nearer future rather than in the more remote future. It operates to limit provision for the future. Ultimately it puts an end to further increases in productive expenditure at the expense of further decreases in the portion of sales revenues used to consume. It also puts an end to any continued lengthening of the time interval between the making of productive expenditures and their appearance as costs in business income statements. At some point, because of time preference, a more distant recovery of a productive expenditure, even with the addition of a given amount of profit, let alone a diminished amount of profit, ceases to be worthwhile, and thus such productive expenditures are not made.

All of this implies that in the long run, net consumption tends to be the only source of profit in the economic system and that the rate of profit tends to be determined by the rate of net consumption alone.

III. 8. Increases in the Quantity of Money and the Perpetuation of Net Investment

Despite the demonstrated tendency of net investment to disappear, leaving the rate of profit based solely on the rate of net consumption and the underlying state of time preference, net investment continues and may account for as much as half of the rate of profit.

What perpetuates the existence of net investment is the increase in the quantity of money and thus the volume of spending in the economic system. When new and additional money enters the economic system, its recipients will sooner or later spend it, The recipients of that spending in turn will re-spend it, and so on and on, so long as the new and additional money remains in existence. As the result of a continuing increase in the quantity of money, the spending and re-spending of money will increase further and further. In an economy with any substantial economic degree of capitalism, very soon, if not immediately, the leading component of this new and additional spending will be productive expenditure.

Inasmuch as productive expenditure increases in the very same instant as new and additional productive expenditures are made, while, except for expensed expenditures, the income-statement costs that result from these additional productive expenditures do not appear for a more or less considerable period of time, an excess of productive expenditure over income-statement costs is perpetuated. For even though, as time goes on, income-statement costs will rise, by the time they rise to equal the larger amount of productive expenditure that brought them into being, productive expenditure will have risen still further, if the increase in the quantity of money and volume of spending continues.

III. 9. The Rate of Increase in the Quantity of Money as a Determinant of the Rate of Profit

Because of the perpetuation of net investment, the rate of profit in the economic system, i.e., the amount of profit divided by the amount of capital invested, will always equal the sum of the rate of net consumption plus the rate of net investment. This, of course, is simply an elaboration of the fact that the rate of profit is the amount of profit divided by the amount of capital, and that the amount of profit is the sum of net consumption plus net investment.

I have demonstrated elsewhere that in the context of an increasing quantity of money and consequent continuing increase in productive expenditure, the rate of net investment that is induced tends to be equal to that very same rate of increase in the quantity of money and volume of spending. For example, a two or three percent annual increase in the quantity of money and volume of spending will tend to result in a two or three percent rate of net investment.[77] Thus, if the rate of profit were four percent or six percent, the half of it that reflected the rate of net investment would be due to nothing more than the increase in the quantity of money and volume of spending,

It is important to realize that with such a comparatively modest rate of increase in the quantity of money and volume of spending, a rate that might result from the use of gold, or gold and silver, as money, the increasing quantity of money and volume of spending could well be accompanied by slowly falling prices. This would be the case, if while the increase in money and spending proceeded at an annual rate of two or three percent, the annual rate of increase in production and supply proceeded at an annual rate of three or four percent, in which case prices would fall each year on the order of one percent.

The fact that increases in the quantity of money and volume of spending tend to add to the rate of profit the same rate as that at which they proceed can be seen in the fact that profit is the difference between two sums of money existing at different points in time: the sum of money expended at one time in order to sell for a larger sum of money at a later time, and that later, larger sum.

Thus assume that with no increase in the quantity of money and volume of spending in the economic system, a merchant would normally buy his goods for $100 and then sell them a year later for $105. But over the course of this year, the quantity of money and volume of spending increase by two percent. As a result, the average seller now sells his goods for two percent more, which means that in this case our average seller sells his goods for $105 x 1.02, which equals $1.07.10, yielding a rate of profit of 7.1 percent instead of 5 percent, i.e., a rate of profit 2.1 percent higher on the capital invested of $100. (The additional one-tenth of a percent added to the rate of profit is the result of the fact that the increase in spending here applies to sales revenues, which, to begin with, were five percent larger than the initial capital invested. If one worked strictly with the increase in net investment, the result would come out to be two percent exactly.[78])

If, initially our merchant were to be able to sell his goods that cost him $100, two years later, for $110.25 (implying a five percent annual rate of profit compounded for two years) and over the course of the intervening two years, the quantity of money and volume of spending increased once again at the rate of two percent per year, our merchant, if he is an average seller, would be able to sell his goods for 1.02^2 times $110.25, or for $114.70, which, once again, reduces to an annual rate of profit of 1.071. Thus, here we have examples of how increases in the quantity of money and volume of spending add at least an approximately equal percentage to the rate of profit and do so irrespective of the length of time that the investment spans.[79]

III. 10. Marxism's/Socialism's Conflict of Hatreds

Marxism/Socialism hates two things: profit and capitalism. It hates profit in the belief that it is stolen from the wage earners, and it hates capitalism in the belief that capitalism is the system that makes this alleged theft possible, through its establishment of capitalistic circulation and alleged enslavement of the wage earners. The Marxists/Socialists are utterly ignorant of the fact that as much as half of the rate of profit is the result of nothing more than the increase in the quantity of money and volume of spending, which at the same time is what serves to perpetuate net investment as a component in the rate of profit, as I have just shown. It is equally unaware that to the extent that this monetary component in the rate of profit exists in an environment of stable or falling prices, it is the accompaniment of an equal or greater annual increase in the production and supply of goods. Thus, to this extent, Marxism's\Socialism's hatred of profit reduces to a hatred of the increase in the quantity of money and volume of spending on the one hand, and the increase in the production and supply of goods on the other. Thus here, Marxism/Socialism is tilting at windmills, for it perceives what is in fact nothing more than increases in money and spending and production and supply as fruits of the "exploitation of labor."

For the rest, Marxism/Socialism is ignorant of the fact that the more fundamental component of profit, net consumption, is the reflection of the extent to which capitalistic circulation is less than one-hundred percent. As I have shown, it is the reflection of the extent to which the sellers of products do not use their sales revenues to make productive expenditures and thus sooner or later create equivalent costs to be deducted from sales revenues, but rather consume those sales revenues. When added to the sales revenues generated by the capitalists' productive expenditure, the sales revenues generated by their consumption expenditure result in total sales revenues greater than productive expenditure and thus greater than the costs productive expenditure generates. So here, it is evident, the generation of the profit that Marxist/Socialists hate and blame on capitalism is the result of the extent to which the capitalists have not acted as capitalists but as consumers. Thus, if the Marxist/Socialists want to see their hate-objects profit and the rate of profit reduced, they must welcome an increase in their hate object capitalism. In the same way, if the Marxist/Socialists want to see their hate-object capitalism reduced, they must welcome an increase in their hate-objects profits and the rate of profit. Marxism/Socialism is a system so filled with hate that it cannot get straight the objects of its hatred and cannot avoid passionately hating something.

This page intentionally left blank.

SUMMARY AND CONCLUSION

For its size, this essay is the most powerful, comprehensive, and in-depth critique of Marxism/Socialism and defense of capitalism ever offered.

It explains why, if socialism, understood as government ownership of the means of production, is to be established, armed robbery and murder on a massive scale are necessary. This requires the communists, who are the true champions of socialism, because only they are willing to commit the bloodshed that is necessary to establish socialism. It argues that so long as the social democrats are unwilling to do this, they should stop calling themselves socialists.

My essay demolishes the attempt of Marxism/Socialism to portray the free workers of capitalism as only nominally free and in actuality slaves.

It demolishes the belief that under what Adam Smith called "the original state of things" and Marx called "simple circulation" profits come into existence as a deduction from wages. It shows instead that *profits exist prior to wages*, by virtue of workers producing and selling products in exchange *not for wages but for sales revenues*. Inasmuch as there are no capitalists present, and thus no buying for the purpose of subsequently selling, there are *no costs* to deduct from these sales revenues, with the result that they are 100 percent *profit*. Then, when capitalists appear, and pay wages and buy capital goods for the purpose of earning sales revenues, their expenditures show up as costs of production to be deducted from sales revenues, thereby reducing the proportion of sales revenues that is profit. Thus capitalists, instead of stealing their profits from wage earners, as the Marxists/Socialists claim, create wages and reduce profits, as well as lay the foundations for continuing economic progress and rising real wages through their purchase and employment of capital goods.

My essay also shows, among many other things, that when it comes to economic planning, capitalism is as rich compared to socialism as it is in the production of material goods. This is because, under capitalism, all participants in the economic system engage in economic planning, with their separate, individual plans being harmonized, coordinated, and integrated by means of the price system. In sharpest contrast, under socialism, economic planning is the monopoly if not of just one man, the Supreme Dictator, then of no more than a relative handful of men, the members of the socialist "central planning board." And while socialism aims at just one economic plan that is binding on everyone and will allegedly be good for several years (recall the 5-Year plans of the Soviet Union and the 4-Year plans of Nazi Germany), the economic plans of capitalism are not only incalculably more numerous, being the plans of hundreds of millions, indeed, of billions of people, but also subject to continuous revision, in response to changing conditions.

As I remarked in my essay, "The alleged economic planning of socialism is in fact not economic planning at all but *the forcible suppression of economic planning*—the forcible suppression of the economic planning of everyone in the economic system outside the membership of the central planning board." And as I also noted, "By its nature, this attempt to make the brains of so few meet the [planning] needs of so many has no more prospect of success than would an attempt to make the legs of so few the vehicle for carrying the weight of so many. To have rational economic planning, the independent thinking and planning of all are required, operating in an environment of private ownership of the means of production and the price system, i.e., capitalism."[80] Absent the economic planning of capitalism, the result is economic chaos, declining production, and starvation. Thus, it is socialism, that cannot maintain its slaves in their slavery and whose workers sink deeper and deeper into poverty, to paraphrase Marx and apply his statements truthfully for once.

Just as my essay presents the truth about socialism, so too does it present the truth about capitalism. For example, it shows how, under capitalism, a willingness of workers to work for minimum subsistence, rather than die of starvation, is irrelevant to the wages they actually need to accept, which are set at a far higher level by the competition of employers for labor. It shows that the actual self-interest of employers is not to try to pay wages that are as low as they might like, but rather the lowest wages that are simultaneously *too high* for any other employers who would otherwise obtain the labor that these employers want to employ. The position of employers under capitalism is essentially the same as that of a successful bidder at an auction. His successful bid must be too high for his next nearest competitor.

Capitalism not only continually raises real wages, i.e., the buying power of wages, based on a combination of capital accumulation and scientific and technological progress, but on the foundation of rising real wages, capitalism also operates to reduce the hours of work, abolish child labor, and improve working conditions. It does this by virtue of the fact that once real wages have increased sufficiently, workers can afford to accept the comparatively lower wages that accompany shorter hours, can afford to keep their children home longer, and can afford to accept the comparatively lower take-home wages that enable employers to provide them with improvements in working conditions that do not pay for themselves through increases in efficiency.

All this, and much more, is contained in the first part of my essay, "The Gist of Marxism/Socialism and Its Refutation."

The second part of my essay, "Marx's Labor Theory of Value Lunacy," deals with major details of Marx's lengthy exposition of his doctrine that profits are stolen from the wage earners—the exploitation theory. As stated at its beginning, it confirms Marx's profound ignorance of economics, his blindness to facts, his intellectual dishonesty, and a pattern of thinking that suggests a series of grudges against capitalists and capitalism manufactured for no other purpose than that of arousing hatred against them and justifying robbing and murdering them.

The third part of my essay, "The Actual Determinants of Profit and the Rate of Profit," is presented as a new and original positive alternative to Marx's doctrine, one whose truth totally precludes Marx's doctrine.

****

Marxism/Socialism has been the dominant politico-economic philosophy of the world for several generations. It is the main set of ideas that underlies hostility to capitalism. The "liberal intellectuals" have taken its validity absolutely for granted and as the starting point of their economic and social programs.[81]

According to them, if not prevented by government intervention, the capitalists would, indeed, set wages at the point of minimum subsistence and the hours of work at the maximum possible limit, in order to maximize their profits. But government intervention, they believe, especially in the form of minimum-wage and prounion legislation, can serve to decree higher wage rates, and all that occurs is that "surplus-labor-time" and "surplus-value" are reduced, thereby equivalently benefitting the wage earners at the expense of the capitalist exploiters' profits. In exactly the same way, the "liberal intellectuals" believe that the government's and the unions' decree of shorter hours also serves merely to reduce "surplus-labor-time" and "surplus-value," again allegedly benefitting the wage earners at the expense of the capitalist exploiters' profits. And, of course, identically the same analysis is present in their arguments for child labor legislation and laws compelling improvements in working conditions. What they believe is that wage rates are set arbitrarily, with the capitalists seeking to set them at or below minimum subsistence and the government, the labor unions, and kind-hearted citizens seeking to set them higher, and that there is nothing else to be concerned with.

With the exploitation theory as their foundation, the "liberal intellectuals'" contribution to the life of their times has been to set about busying themselves both with the critique of the capitalist society in which they have lived, and with the concoction of all manner of schemes and programs for overcoming the various evils that the exploitation theory in its flights of fancy absurdly and maliciously attributes to capitalism. They have bent art and literature, history and journalism, philosophy and science, and politics, law, and government, to conform with the exploitation theory and its ludicrous implications.

When the absurdities of the exploitation theory are fully understood, it becomes clear that never in all of human history has a greater bunch of pompous ignoramuses with pretensions to knowledge behaved more destructively and self-destructively—made themselves more a spectacle of downright fools meriting the utter contempt of all mankind—than have the "liberal intellectuals" of the last several generations. Their lack of genuine liberalism is surpassed only by their lack of genuine intellect.

ROYALTY-FREE DISTRIBUTION OF COPIES

Note: the author wants to encourage readership of this essay. Write to him at greisman1937@gmail.com to receive a free copy that you can duplicate and distribute either as an email attachment file or in hardcopy format (or both). This permission requires that there be no charge to the recipients and that the essay be distributed in full, without any part of it being changed or deleted, If you wish to add any comments of your own, you are welcome to do so, but in a separate document, either under your own name or marked anonymous but in no case ascribed to George Reisman. Extremely worthwhile targets are students, academics, opinion makers such as authors and journalists, politicians, legislators and their staffs, and government officials.

This page intentionally left blank.

ACKNOWLEDGEMENTS

I want to acknowledge here my indebtedness to my late mentor Ludwig von Mises, who was the first man in history to present a clear, comprehensive and powerful in-depth defense of capitalism and critique of socialism. Most of the arguments I raise are either his or are inspired by him. I also wish to acknowledge the influence of Ayn Rand, especially for my ability to refute the Marxist/Socialist attempt to portray freedom as slavery.

I need to note that the role of capitalists' consumption and gross investment in the determination of aggregate profit in the economic system was recognized by two twentieth-century economists of the far left: the Polish economist Michael Kalecki and the British economist Joan Robinson. However, apart from identification of these two components (in my case, of course, net investment, not gross investment) and the fact that their sum equals aggregate profit, there is little in common between us either in the development or in the application of these concepts.[82]

This page intentionally left blank.

POSTSCRIPT

The content of this essay is mainly based on, and frequently taken from, the author's magnum opus *Capitalism: A Treatise on Economics,* especially, Chapters 6-9, 11, and 13-18. If you someday want to be an intellectual leader in the fight against Marxism/Socialism and for capitalism, this book is essential reading. For an indication of its overall scope, here is its table of contents in brief (the full, detailed table of contents is almost thirty pages long). The book is available on Amazon.com at https://amzn.to/2xOrJxI .

CONTENTS IN BRIEF

PREFACE xxxix

INTRODUCTION 1

PART ONE

THE FOUNDATIONS OF ECONOMICS

CHAPTER 1. ECONOMICS AND CAPITALISM 15

CHAPTER 2. WEALTH AND ITS ROLE IN HUMAN LIFE 39

CHAPTER 3. NATURAL RESOURCES AND THE ENVIRONMENT 63

PART TWO

THE DIVISION OF LABOR AND CAPITALISM

CHAPTER 4. THE DIVISION OF LABOR AND PRODUCTION 123

CHAPTER 5. THE DEPENDENCE OF THE DIVISION OF LABOR ON CAPITALISM I 135

CHAPTER 6. THE DEPENDENCE OF THE DIVISION OF LABOR ON CAPITALISM II: THE PRICE SYSTEM AND ECONOMIC COORDINATION 172

CHAPTER 7. THE DEPENDENCE OF THE DIVISION OF LABOR ON CAPITALISM III: PRICE CONTROLS AND ECONOMIC CHAOS 219

CHAPTER 8. THE DEPENDENCE OF THE DIVISION OF LABOR ON CAPITALISM IV: SOCIALISM, ECONOMIC CHAOS, AND TOTALITARIAN DICTATORSHIP 267

CHAPTER 9. THE INFLUENCE OF THE DIVISION OF LABOR ON THE INSTITUTIONS OF CAPITALISM 296

CHAPTER 10. MONOPOLY VERSUS FREEDOM OF COMPETITION 375

CHAPTER 11. THE DIVISION OF LABOR AND THE CONCEPT OF PRODUCTIVE ACTIVITY 441

PART THREE

THE PROCESS OF ECONOMIC PROGRESS

CHAPTER 12. MONEY AND SPENDING 503

CHAPTER 13. PRODUCTIONISM, SAY'S LAW, AND UNEMPLOYMENT 542

CHAPTER 14. THE PRODUCTIVITY THEORY OF WAGES 603

CHAPTER 15. AGGREGATE PRODUCTION, AGGREGATE SPENDING, AND THE

ROLE OF SAVING IN SPENDING 673

CHAPTER 16. THE NET-CONSUMPTION/NET-INVESTMENT THEORY OF PROFIT AND INTEREST 719

CHAPTER 17. APPLICATIONS OF THE INVARIABLE-MONEY/NET-CONSUMPTION ANALYSIS 809

CHAPTER 18. KEYNESIANISM: A CRITIQUE 863

CHAPTER 19. GOLD VERSUS INFLATION 895

EPILOGUE

CHAPTER 20. TOWARD THE ESTABLISHMENT OF LAISSEZ-FAIRE CAPITALISM 969

A BIBLIOGRAPHY OF WRITINGS IN DEFENSE OF CAPITALISM 991

INDEX 999

This page intentionally left blank.

NOTES

[1] See https://nyti.ms/2r9pP4k.

[2] R. J. Rummel, *Death By Government* (New Brunswick, N.J., Transaction Publishers, 1994), n. 1.

[3] Socialism can also be established through fraud, under the outward guise and appearance of capitalism. This is the case when the government controls prices and wages and decides what is to be produced, in what quantities, by what methods, and to whom the products are to be distributed. In this case, the government exercises all of the essential powers of ownership and is thus the de facto owner of the means of production. In the words of Ludwig von Mises, this is socialism on the German or Nazi pattern, in contrast to the open, de jure Russian or Bolshevik pattern of socialism.

[4] Cf. Daniel Lacalle, "Face It, Nordic Countries Aren't Socialist," at https://mises.org/wire/face-it-nordic-countries-arent-socialist

[5] See https://bit.ly/2lmAXIE, paragraph three.

[6] George Orwell had their number down perfectly in his classic *1984*.

[7] See Karl Marx, *Capital*, trans. from 3d German ed. by Samuel Moore and Edward Aveling; Frederick Engels, ed.; rev. and amplified according to the 4th German ed. by Ernest Untermann (New York: 1906), vol. 1; (reprinted, New York: Random House, The Modern Library), pp. 41-848. Hereafter this work will be cited as *Capital*, vol. 1.

References to the Modern Library Edition will appear in brackets.

[8] John Kenneth Galbraith, *The New Industrial State*, 2d ed. rev. (New York: New American Library, 1971), p. 141.

[9] Adam Smith, *Wealth of Nations*, bk. 1, chap. 8.

[10] Ibid., bk. 1, chap. 6.

[11] Now in fact there easily could be an exploitation of labor under "simple circulation"—a genuine, real-life exploitation of labor, based on a rational definition of exploitation. For example, some men could seize other men, force them to produce commodities for sale in the market, and then use the proceeds for their own benefit, not for the workers' benefit, or, to make the arrangement sustainable, leave just enough for the workers to stay alive and have the strength to continue to work. This, in fact, would be slavery, genuine slavery. However, I will not belabor this point, even though it's enough to call into question Marx's very starting point, which is to present the sequence C-M-C as representing the absence of the exploitation of labor.

[12] Marx, *Capital*, vol. 1, pt. II, chap. IV, pp. 163-173.

[13] John Stuart Mill, *Principles of Political Economy*, Ashley ed. (1909; reprint ed., Fairfield, N. J.: Augustus M. Kelley, 1976), pp. 79–81. See also the author's *Capitalism: A Treatise on Economics* (Laguna Hills, California: TJS Books, 2009; Kindle Edition, 2012), especially pp. 683-689. The author's book is hereafter referred to simply as *Capitalism*.

[14] For further explanation and development of this point, see below, pp. 98-101.

[15] Indeed, capitalists are not only the source of the demand for the labor that wage earners sell, but also of the supply of products that wage earners buy. On this point, see idem. Apart from a few minor changes, this and the preceding paragraph appear on p. 479 of *Capitalism*.]

[16] F. A. Hayek, *Capitalism and the Historians* (Chicago: University of Chicago Press, 1954), pp. 15, 16. This paragraph too appears on p. 479 of *Capitalism*.

[17] On the connection between capitalistic circulation and division of labor, see below, pp. 42-44.

[18] *Wealth of Nations,* bk. 1, chap. 6.

[19] On the subject of having no accumulated capital to steal, see above, p 8.

[20] With minor changes, this section is taken from *Capitalism,* pp. 613-617.

[21] In contrast to Marx, the "iron law of wages" propounded by the classical economists was not based on any claim of an arbitrary power of employers to set wages at minimum subsistence. Wages at minimum subsistence was held to be the result of population growth, which, to feed the larger number of people, would require resort to the cultivation of progressively inferior lands and the more intensive cultivation of lands already under cultivation, either of which would result in a falling output of agricultural commodities relative to the number of workers. The same was held to be true in mining. This was held to reduce the

buying power of wages as population increased and would go on until real wages were so low that workers could not afford to raise more children than were sufficient to prevent depopulation. This belief was descriptive of events prior to the nineteenth century, and from the perspective of the early nineteenth century appeared to be proved by economic history. Even so, Ricardo, the greatest of the classical economists could observe in 1821 that the operation of this "law" could be counteracted by continued capital accumulation. (David Ricardo, *Principles of Political Economy and Taxation*, 3d ed. (London, 1821), chap. V.)

[22] The convention in economics is to talk of supply and demand "curves" and to refer even to straight lines as "curves."

[23] See Eugen von Böhm-Bawerk, Capital and Interest, 3 vols., trans. George D. Huncke and Hans F. Sennholz (South Holland,Ill.: Libertarian Press, 1959), 2:245. See also Capitalism, pp. 162–163.

[24] See *Capitalism*, p. 204.

[25] See ibid., p. 59 and pp. 63–70.

[26] Full employment, it should be realized, is consistent with many workers voluntarily choosing to remain unemployed while they search for particular job opportunities. In addition, full employment need not mean full employment throughout the economic system. The principle applies occupation by occupation, location by location. Thus, for example, the wage rates of house painters in Indianapolis cannot fall below the point of full employment of house

painters in Indianapolis, irrespective of the state of employment in other locations or occupations.

[27] With minor changes, this and the following paragraph are taken from pages 617 and 618 of *Capitalism*.

[28] See ibid., pp. 584–585. For a full discussion of unemployment and real wages, see ibid., pp. 580-602.

[29] This outcome finds additional support in the fact that the achievement of full employment is accompanied by a *rise* in the productivity of labor insofar as the additional employees preponderantly perform direct labor rather than administrative labor. For elaboration of this point, see ibid., p. 586.

[30] For explanation of this vital fact, see the next section "How Capitalism Progressively Raises Real Wages."

[31] This doctrine, including all of its alleged relationships, is taught under the name "the IS curve." For a full, exposition and critique of Keynes' doctrine on unemployment, see *Capitalism*, chap. 18, pp. 863-894.

[32] To the extent that sales revenues exceed productive expenditure, profit exceeds net investment. For elaboration, see below, pp. 89-107.

[33] In the light of what has just been established, Adam Smith's claim that "Had this state continued [i.e., the state "which precedes both the appropriation of land and the accumulation of stock"], the wages of labour would have augmented with all those improvements in its productive powers, to which the division of labour gives occasion" appears absurd. The fact is that in the absence of

capitalistic circulation there would have been very little division of labor indeed, and thus virtually no improvements in the productive powers of labor dependent on the division of labor or on other aspects of capitalistic circulation.

[34] See above, pp. 18-21.

[35] It is important to note that under capitalism, great fortunes are accumulated by introducing a series of major innovations. The innovations earn high rates of profit the great bulk of which is saved and reinvested. The combination of a high rate of profit with high saving and reinvestment of that profit, is the source of rapid accumulation of capital. Repeated innovations are necessary because competition serves to erode the profits on any given innovation. And, of course, the capitals accumulated are the source both of the supply of products that nonowners of the means of production buy and of the demand for the labor that the nonowners of the means of production sell. For elaboration, see the author's *How the 1 Percent Provides the Standard of Living of the 99 Percent*, available from Amazon.com at https://www.amzn.to/2tKVz1X. For the most complete treatment, see the author's *Capitalism*, pp. 176-180 and 326-332.

[36] These two sentences are taken from point 11 of the author's essay "Some Fundamental Insights into the Benevolent Nature of Capitalism."

[37] For elaboration of this essential point, see *Capitalism*, pp. 269-275.

[38] The immediate cause of universal shortages under open, Russian-style socialism is the quota system, which sets minimum output levels that every establishment is compelled to meet and encouraged to exceed by as much as possible. It is impossible to have resources sufficient to meet the simultaneous attempts of all users of the resources to use more of them without limit. The reason for the quota system itself is that socialism, not having a price system, and thus no possibility of using the standard of profit and loss, which it considers immoral in any case, has no alternative but simply to try to produce as much as possible—of everything.

[39] See *Capitalism*, pp. 286-288.

[40] The following ten paragraphs are taken from pp. 284-285 of *Capitalism*. They also appear in the author's essay "Why Nazism Was Socialism and Why Socialism Is Totalitarian."

[41] The material in this section comes from p. 290 of *Capitalism*.

[42] See Hedrick Smith, *The Russians* (New York: Quadrangle/New York Times Book Company, 1976), p. 265. For elaboration of this point, see p. 286 of *Capitalism* and the text of note 27 on pp. 294-295.

[43] For a critique of Marx on all of these points, see *Capitalism,* pp. 487-490.

[44] Marx, *Capital*, vol. 1, pt. 1, chap. 1 [p. 46]. The sentence in quotation marks is from an earlier work by Marx himself, namely, his *Critique of Political Economy*, published in 1859.

[45] Ibid., sec. 2 [pp. 51–52].

[46] Marx, *Capital*, vol. 1, pt. 2, chap. 6 [pp. 189–190]. See also above, Part I, the section "The Marxists/Socialists' Rationalization for the Armed Robbery Needed to Establish Socialism: Alleged 'Exploitation' and 'Wage Slavery' under Capitalism."

[47] See above, note 21, which discusses the essentially loose connection that the classical economists, looking back at economic history from the perspective of the early nineteenth century, believed existed between wages and subsistence.

[48] Marx, *Capital*, ibid. pt. 4, chap. 12 [pp. 350–351].

[49] See above, pp. 26-39.

[50] See above, pp. 75f.

[51] See above, pp. 53-55.

[52] Marx, *Capital,* vol. 1, pt. 3, chap. 10, sec. 1 [p. 257], sec. 2 [p. 260].

[53] Ibid., chap. 8, [pp. 232-233.]. The chapter is titled "Constant Capital and Variable Capital."

[54] Karl Marx, *Capital*, 3 vols. (Moscow: Foreign Languages Publishing House, 1962), 3:207–209.

[55] For elaboration of this very important principle, see the author's *Capitalism*, pp. 172-187.

[56] Cf. David Ricardo, *Principles of Political Economy and Taxation,* 3d. ed. (London, 1821), chap. I, sec. IV.

[57] Marx, *Theories of Surplus Value*, trans. by G. A, Bonner and Emile Burns (London, 1951), pp. 208-342. This book was intended by Marx to be Volume IV of *Capital*.

[58] "s/v" stands for "surplus-value divided by "variable capital."

[59] This paragraph appears on p. 612 of the author's *Capitalism*.

[60] Marx, *Capital*, vol. 1, pt. 3, chap. 10, sec. 5 [pp. 290–292].

[61] See above, pp. 48-52.

[62] This paragraph too appears on p. 612 of the author's *Capitalism*.

[63] Marx, *Capital*, vol. 1, pt. 4, chap. 15, sec. 3, subsec. a [pp. 431–432].

[64] Marx's actual example is in terms of English shillings and is unnecessarily complicated by his assumption that each shilling of product value corresponds to two hours of labor in the production of the product, instead of just one.

[65] Again, see above, pp. 48-52.

[66] Marx, *Capital*, vol. 1, pt. 7, chap. 24, sec. 4 [pp. 658–659].

[67] With minor changes, this paragraph is taken from p. 608 of the author's *Capitalism*.

[68] In the conditions of "simple circulation," cash held by sellers does not constitute capital, for it is not held for the

purpose of making subsequent productive expenditures or for any kind of business purpose. It is a consumer cash holding, not a business cash holding.

[69] See above, pp. 15-18.

[70] Cf. Böhm-Bawerk, *Capital and Interest*, 1:263–271. See also *Capitalism*, pp. 484-485.

[71] See above, pp. 42-48.

[72] For more on the concept of consumers' labor, see *Capitalism*, pp. 446-447 and p. 456.

[73] Ironically, capitalism so enriches wage earners that they too become able to save and invest and thus become capitalists on some scale. However, the savings of wage earners tend ultimately to be consumed, as in such cases as saving up to buy expensive consumers' goods or to provide funds to be available for consumption in illness or retirement. Thus over a sufficiently long period, virtually all of wage earners' current savings tend to be consumed, with the saving of wage earners in the present being accompanied by the consumption, on the part of other wage earners, of savings accumulated in the past. Of course, even if current overall net saving on the part of wage earners becomes zero, their accumulated savings would still be of great importance and would be permanent, as the dissaving of older workers, would be matched by the fresh saving of younger workers.

[74] This, of course, brings us back to Mill's proposition that "demand for commodities is not demand for labor." For it was precisely this essential fact about profits that I offered in defense of his proposition. And it was his proposition

that opened up the realization that profit, not wages, is the original, primary form of labor income. See above, pp. 15-18.

[75] Inasmuch as equals added to unequals do not affect the amount of the inequality, it is also correct to express net consumption as the difference simply between consumption expenditure in the economic system and wage payments in the economic system. This is because the addition of the expenditure for consumers' labor—i.e., labor employed not for the purpose of making subsequent sales—to the expenditure for consumers' goods raises the latter to total consumption expenditure, while its addition to the expenditure for producers' labor results in the total expenditure for labor.

[76] See *Capitalism*, pp. 719-862 for the full development and application of this concept.

[77] Ibid., pp. 762-774.

[78] See idem.

[79] It is remarkable that something so important and at the same time so simple as the role of increases in the quantity of money and volume of spending in the determination of the rate of profit could have been almost entirely overlooked until I presented it in *Capitalism* and here present it again. The only connection between more money and spending on the one side and the rate of profit on the other, that has been recognized, has been in the case of rising prices, which has been widely acknowledged as being accompanied by artificially inflated profits. But there has apparently been no previous identification of the role of increases in the quantity of money and volume of spending

as a regular and substantial contributor to the rate of profit in normal circumstances, in which the increase in the quantity of money and volume of spending would exist within the limits of the increase in the production and supply of goods and add to the rate of profit in that context.

[80] See above, pp. 57-63.

[81] The substance of this sentence has been taken from page 613 of *Capitalism,* as have the next three paragraphs, with minor revisions.

[82] For elaboration, see ibid., pp. 801-803.

Made in the USA
Middletown, DE
05 October 2018